(TGV)

£10 —

TM

21/3.

(8)

THE VICTORIA HISTORY
OF THE
COUNTIES OF ENGLAND

—

GENERAL
INTRODUCTION:
SUPPLEMENT 1970–90

Oxford University Press, Walton Street, Oxford OX2 6DP
Oxford New York Toronto
Delhi Bombay Calcutta Madras Karachi
Petaling Jaya Singapore Hong Kong Tokyo
Nairobi Dar es Salaam Cape Town
Melbourne Auckland

and associated companies in
Berlin Ibadan

Oxford is a trade mark of Oxford University Press

Published in the United States
by Oxford University Press, New York

British Library Cataloguing in Publication Data
The Victoria history of the counties of England:
general introduction: supplement, 1970–90.
1. Great Britain. Countries, history
I. Elrington, C. R. (Christopher Robin), 1930–
II. University of London
Institute of Historical Research
941
ISBN 0 19 722777 5

Distributed by Oxford University Press until 1 January 1993
thereafter by Dawsons of Pall Mall

Typeset at the University of London Computer Centre
Printed in Great Britain by The Bath Press, Avon

THE VICTORIA HISTORY
OF THE
COUNTIES OF ENGLAND

EDITED BY C. R. ELRINGTON

THE UNIVERSITY OF LONDON
INSTITUTE OF
HISTORICAL RESEARCH

INSCRIBED TO THE

MEMORY OF HER LATE MAJESTY

QUEEN VICTORIA

WHO GRACIOUSLY GAVE THE TITLE TO

AND ACCEPTED THE DEDICATION

OF THIS HISTORY

THE VICTORIA HISTORY
OF THE
COUNTIES OF ENGLAND

GENERAL INTRODUCTION: SUPPLEMENT 1970–90

EDITED BY C. R. ELRINGTON

PUBLISHED FOR

THE INSTITUTE OF HISTORICAL RESEARCH

BY

OXFORD UNIVERSITY PRESS

1990

CONTENTS

PAGE

Dedication iv

Contents vii

Editorial Note ix

The Victoria County History 1970–90 1

State of the V.C.H. (at December 1990) 9

   Counties completed, in progress, dormant, and unstarted . . . 9

   Counties in progress and dormant: work published, in progress,
   and to be started 9

Lists of Contents of Volumes published 1971–90 15

Index of Titles of Articles 57

Index of Authors 65

Corrigenda to the *General Introduction* 67

EDITORIAL NOTE

When in 1970 the *Victoria History* had published one hundred and fifty volumes, a *General Introduction* was issued. It contained an account of the Origin and Progress of the History, a Bibliographical Note, the lists of contents from the volumes (other than index volumes), and indexes of the titles of articles and of authors. Those constituent parts make it a useful guide to the series but one which has become progressively out of date. Twenty years and about fifty volumes on, it is appropriate to publish a supplement. The main purpose is to list the contents of the volumes published since 1970 and to index the titles and authors of the articles; at the same time the supplement records changes in the structure and organization of the *Victoria History* and gives some guidance to the reader in the use of its volumes.

The arrangement of the *General Introduction* of 1970 has largely determined that of the present supplement. The main difference is that the supplement omits a bibliographical note, and instead includes the name of the editor of each volume and the date of publication along with the lists of contents; the supplement also includes a summary list for all the counties, showing for those that are incomplete the nature of the contents of each published volume and what remains to be published.

THE VICTORIA COUNTY
HISTORY 1970–1990

The Character of the V.C.H.

The V.C.H. is essentially a scholarly work of reference. The character of the series was set in its early years, and while there have been and will continue to be improvements and modifications, the main features are retained in order to preserve the integrity of the series; to introduce far-reaching changes in the selection, arrangement, and presentation of material would be in effect to start a new series.

It is axiomatic that a scholarly work of reference should be comprehensive, factual, reliable, and unbiased. It must be based on original research rather than on the repetition of earlier work, and where possible the research must be in primary sources. One requirement of scholarship is that the information which is presented should be firmly linked to the sources from which it is drawn, and in the V.C.H. that is done by the use of numerous footnotes. The assumption is that every statement except those based on contemporary observation is supported by the sources cited in the footnote whose number follows the statement in the text.

An historical work on such a large scale is necessarily a long-term enterprise, even without practical difficulties of the sort which from time to time the V.C.H. has faced and without the limitation of its resources. The V.C.H. has been at work now for more than ninety years and even so (given the much enlarged scope of its town and parish histories) it is less than half way through the task which its founders set themselves. Over so long a period successive editors have had to strive to ensure some consistency of approach to local history and to adhere to a systematic presentation which not only maintains the character of the series but also makes it possible for the reader to make comparisons from county to county and from parish to parish. They have introduced new topics and tried new methods, but not in response to changing fashions or personal inclinations.

In addition to those constraints on the authors and editors of the V.C.H. are the limitations of time and space. By the standards of academic research or of publishing, the V.C.H. is a very large undertaking, and like most large undertakings it feels the need to grow bigger and has to be controlled. Research tends to exceed the time allotted to it, and authors tend, particularly when their prolonged research has yielded more than was expected, to write more than they have been asked for. The progressive enlargement of the V.C.H. parish history, in the amount of time and the number of words or pages that it takes, was discussed in 1970,[1] and the tendency towards enlargement did not cease then. The subject matter of local history continues to expand, the amount of source material available increases year by year, and the period to be covered ever lengthens.

[1] *V.C.H. General Introduction*, 26–7.

Nevertheless, editors cannot allow the content of the V.C.H. to expand unchecked. Increased time in compilation requires increased expenditure; larger or more numerous volumes cost more, take more shelf space, and make it harder to find any particular piece of information; above all, more time and greater length defer the publication of a given volume and the finishing of a county's history. The completion of the series, though a long and incalculable time away, is the ultimate aim, since only when the series is complete will its comprehensive character and the comparability which it offers be fulfilled.

The V.C.H. seeks to serve a great variety of uses. Few readers other than reviewers will read a volume through from beginning to end, and not many other than local residents will read even a town or parish history right through. Local residents, whose loyalties make any information about a place relevant and fascinating for them, represent one end of the spectrum of the readership. At the other end are the academic historians who want to know how the local manifestations of historical phenomena help to resolve the problems or illustrate the themes with which they are concerned. The V.C.H. aims to help readers at both ends and many in between. Most readers, having neither local loyalties nor an academic concern with history, go to the volumes to find information about a particular person, family, institution, building, or aspect of county, town, parish, or village history. The intention is to cover all aspects, and emphasis on any one aspect or approach inevitably means the comparative neglect of others. At the same time, the need for reliability and impartiality works against colour and liveliness of presentation, the demands of economy discourage illuminating anecdote and revealing detail, and the systematic structure of the series imposes a pattern with little variation. The V.C.H. chooses to sacrifice some of the excitement of local history in its attempt to serve many purposes within constricted limits. In trying to meet a wide range of needs, it assumes that those who turn to its pages do not need to have their interest in history aroused or to be persuaded of the relevance of the subject matter.

The V.C.H. and its Readers

In using the V.C.H. readers will find it helpful to remember that each volume and each article is part of a series; because of the need for economy in presentation the V.C.H. avoids unnecessary repetition. If the information which the reader wants is not in a particular article it may be in another article, another volume for the county, or a volume for another county. Since the series is far from complete, it may be that the information required has yet to be published.

The long-running nature of the series has resulted (notwithstanding what has been written above) in unevenness of treatment. A few features found in the early volumes are missing from later ones; a larger number of features, and particularly the greater fullness of parish and town histories, in the later volumes are missing from the early ones. In particular, the writers of the early volumes were using a much more restricted range of sources than that available to their successors today.

The counties into which the series is divided are essentially the historic counties but with some adjustments. For each county the volumes are divided between general chapters on aspects of county history and topographical chapters giving the separate history of every town and parish. The main aspects of county

history covered by the general chapters are: natural history (omitted from volumes published after 1950 except for geological physique), prehistory, the Roman period, the Anglo-Saxon period, Domesday, political and administrative history, ecclesiastical history, religious houses, economic and social history, endowed schools, and sport. In the topographical chapters the history of each town and parish is divided by topics: following an introductory section there have from the beginning been regular sections on the manor or manors, the church, and charities for the poor. In volumes published since about 1950 there have additionally been regular sections on economic history, local government, nonconformity, and schools; moreover, notable estates that were not manors have been added (in most parishes) to manors.

The parishes are usually arranged in the volumes according to the hundreds or wapentakes (the ancient administrative divisions of the county) in which they lay. For each county the V.C.H. sets out the composition of the hundreds or wapentakes in the Population Table that is included among the general chapters.[2]

The footnotes serve as a guide to sources of information. While the V.C.H. cannot be exhaustive, readers are intended to treat it as a starting point for further inquiry and research, providing both a basis of verifiable fact and an indication of where further detail is to be found. The references which the footnotes contain are often highly abbreviated: in the more recent volumes they are mostly interpreted in the preliminary pages.

The V.C.H. aims to show in what ways a county, a part of it, or a parish differs from other places. It is not possible, place by place, to define the many characteristics which large numbers of places have in common. Equally, it would be impracticable to explain, place by place, the historical background or to define recurrent terms of a more or less technical sort. The reader who does not understand, in reading about the ownership of land, words like copyhold, disseise, dower, enfeoff, holding by the curtesy, and wardship, or, in reading about the measurement of land, words like hide, carucate and ploughland, virgate and yardland, is expected to consult a dictionary: the V.C.H. does not explain words that are adequately defined in the *Shorter Oxford Dictionary*. It will tell the reader about the local characteristics of copyhold or the number of acres in a yardland on a given manor, but it assumes a general understanding of the words. It assumes, also, that the reader will be aware that the authors of the V.C.H. use words and phrases with care, to express precise meanings; it may be obvious that a vicar, for example, is distinct from a rector but less obvious that hamlet, tithing, and township are separate though possibly overlapping entities. For the general background the reader may usefully consult W. G. Hoskins's *Local History in England* (3rd edn. 1984) or Philip Riden's *Local History: a Handbook for Beginners* (1983). Two older books are useful for understanding parish history: R. B. Pugh's *How to Write a Parish History* (1954, described as the 6th edn. of J. C. Cox's book of the same name of 1879 but in fact a new work) is especially relevant because its author was general editor of the V.C.H.; W. E. Tate's *The Parish Chest* (3rd edn. 1969) discusses many aspects and details of parish administration.

---

[2] The only county for which the V.C.H. has published topographical chapters but no Population Table is Northamptonshire. It has yet to publish Population Tables also for Cornwall, Cumberland, Devonshire, Herefordshire, Norfolk, Northumberland, and Westmorland. The Population Table for London is in *V.C.H. Mdx.* ii.

The Progress of the V.C.H. 1970–90

In the twenty years since 1970, nearly one fifth of its whole existence, the V.C.H. has undergone, in proportion, many fewer ups and downs than in its first seven decades. In those two decades local history has grown greatly in the number of its practitioners and in the range of its sources and subject matter. While the V.C.H. has provided for many local historians a starting point and a standard of scholarly discipline, it is perhaps to be expected that what is essentially an encyclopaedic work of reference, always struggling with the problem of presenting *multum in parvo*, should follow and reflect new ideas rather than pioneer them. The reader who compares V.C.H. volumes published in 1970 and 1990 will find more attention given in the later volumes to landscape history and to the evolution of settlement, a change which is evident partly from the inclusion of a much greater number of maps. An awareness of regional history, which the sceptical may think means little more than grouping the smaller counties together and dividing the larger ones, is to some extent represented by the inclusion in topographical volumes of introductory sections bringing together scattered themes.

Emphases in architectural history keep changing. When the Royal Commission on Historical Monuments (England) abandoned the preparation of the traditional inventories it presented a challenge to which the V.C.H. is unable fully to respond. From the 1940s it had been the assumption that, since the R.C.H.M. would in due time publish a description of each building of historical importance, the V.C.H. could limit itself to a brief mention of the main features and the use of the building as a piece of evidence. The assumption has now been made false, but the V.C.H. has neither the staff nor the space within its already well filled volumes to describe buildings in detail.

The policy of the V.C.H. is to persevere with traditional practices until they are shown to be pointless and not to adopt new ones until they have shown their worth. That Editions Alecto in the facsimile edition of Domesday Book has based its new translations of each county section on those published in the V.C.H. over many years may show the value of keeping to established ways. A recurrent complaint, though a minor one, about V.C.H. topographical volumes is that they group the parishes according to the ancient and obsolete hundreds; about 1970 it was often asked why parishes were not grouped by rural districts. The answer then was that the hundreds had lasted for a thousand years while the rural districts were subject to change and had yet to survive a century. The rural districts have now gone, combined into new districts; it may also be noted that they derived from rural sanitary districts, which in turn derived from poor-law unions, and that the unions were in most instances based on the hundreds. To make the areas covered by topographical volumes more immediately recognizable to readers unfamiliar with the historical divisions of a county, the practice of giving each volume a subtitle has been increasingly used.

The modernization of the V.C.H. most apparent to those involved in its compilation is the use of word-processors. In addition to all the advantages which they have in editing, word-processors enable the volumes to be typeset from the author's or editor's disk. That greatly reduces the cost of production and therefore the retail price. While V.C.H. volumes will never be cheap, the price of new

volumes did not rise with inflation between 1982 and 1990, and the use of word-processors should help to limit future increases.

Most of the work of the V.C.H. in recent years has been towards the compilation of topographical volumes, telling the history of particular places, rather than of general volumes: of the fifty volumes published since 1970, forty are topographical. A high proportion of the topographical volumes relates to urban history: six of them are devoted to cities or major towns (Beverley, Gloucester, Oxford, Stafford, Telford, and part of the West Midlands conurbation in Staffordshire), eight cover parts of Essex and Middlesex that have become London suburbs, and ten include the histories of towns of local importance (Banbury, Brentwood, Bridlington, Crawley, Devizes, Harlow, Horsham, Marlborough, Stroud, Woodstock, and Worthing). The fourteen volumes now in preparation include two general volumes (for Gloucestershire and Shropshire) and topographical volumes on Chester, Colchester, Lichfield, and parishes in Middlesex forming part of the East End of London.

In the structure and organization of the series there was between 1970 and 1990 no fundamental change. Immediately before the rapid price inflation of the mid seventies the financial resources and staffing of the V.C.H. expanded in a modest way, and thereafter underwent a period of consolidation.

Two further counties joined the ten on which the V.C.H. was working in 1970.[3] Cheshire, for which the V.C.H. had until then published no volume, was brought into the fold by the initiative of the Leverhulme Trust. In 1972 the late Professor Alec Myers of Liverpool University prompted the Trust to offer a grant equivalent to half the estimated cost of the Cheshire V.C.H. for seven years provided that another source could be found for the rest of the cost and for the whole cost from the end of the seven years. The Cheshire County Council generously took on that commitment, and a county editor and an assistant were appointed. The administrative arrangements differed from those then in effect in other counties: the editorial staff were employed by the University of London, using the money provided by the Trust and the County Council; similar arrangements were later adopted for three other counties where the V.C.H. was already in progress. In Cheshire the County Council soon found itself, as a result of inflation and rising salaries, paying much more than half the cost of the Cheshire V.C.H. even though the Trust renewed its grant for a further eight years and increased the amount.

The other county was Sussex, on which the V.C.H. had done no significant work since 1953. The completion of the Warwickshire V.C.H. in 1969 left the central staff with some spare capacity, and the central V.C.H. Committee decided to resume work on Sussex. The West Sussex County Council, whose Chief Executive Mr. G. C. Godber was a member of that committee and had been instrumental in restarting the Shropshire V.C.H., then offered to speed progress by paying for an editor, who was to be employed by London University in the same way as the Cheshire editorial staff.

The Middlesex V.C.H. had been resumed in 1955 by a committee representing the Local Authorities in what was then the administrative county. Although that county ceased to exist under the London Government Act of 1963, the volumes

[3] Cambridgeshire, Essex, Gloucestershire, Middlesex, Oxfordshire, Shropshire, Somerset, Staffordshire, Wiltshire, the East Riding of Yorkshire.

of the V.C.H. which related to its area were carried through to completion under the sponsorship of the successor Authorities.[4] Meanwhile the seven London Boroughs[5] in what was historically part of Middlesex but within the area of the former London County Council formed a new committee which in 1980 assumed responsibility for the continuation of the Middlesex history, employing the same editorial staff. Though less radically than Middlesex, Essex was also affected by the London Government Act, its metropolitan south-west corner being transferred to Greater London, but the five London Boroughs concerned[6] have continued most generously to support the Essex V.C.H.; the other sponsors in Essex were formerly the District Councils in the administrative county, but in 1977 the Essex County Council took over their share of the burden.

The Local Government Act of 1972 redrew the English county boundaries, and the consequences for the V.C.H. could have been grave. Of the ten counties away from London whose histories were then in progress, the two least affected by boundary changes were Shropshire and Wiltshire. In Sussex part of what had been East Sussex was transferred to West Sussex. Parts of north Cheshire were placed in the metropolitan counties of Greater Manchester and Merseyside, and part of south Staffordshire in that of the West Midlands; changes were made in the composition and financial arrangements of the Staffordshire V.C.H. Committee. The Act enlarged Oxfordshire and Cambridgeshire as administrative counties, but in each instance the added areas (respectively part of Berkshire, and Huntingdonshire and the soke of Peterborough) had already been covered by the V.C.H. The most difficult problems which the Act posed for the V.C.H. related to the new county of Avon, comprising parts of Gloucestershire and Somerset, and the East Riding of Yorkshire. To those actively concerned with the V.C.H. it was quite clear that its division of the country into counties could not be adjusted to accord with the new counties created by the Act, partly because the old counties had been in existence for far longer and partly because many volumes had already been written and published on the basis of the old counties. The County Councils of Gloucestershire and Somerset, reduced in area and in sources of income, continue to sponsor the V.C.H. within their more limited boundaries. It is hoped that the towns and parishes in Avon will eventually be included in volumes of the Gloucestershire and the Somerset V.C.H., but the Avon County Council has expressed itself as unwilling, for understandable reasons, to sponsor the V.C.H. unless it was called the history of Avon.

The East Riding V.C.H. had been sponsored jointly by the East Riding County Council, the Corporation of Kingston upon Hull, and the Corporation of the City of York. In 1970, the year after the history of Hull had been published as *East Riding* Volume I (the history of York, which was in no riding, had earlier been published simply as *York* and not as part of the East Riding set), Hull Corporation withdrew from the East Riding V.C.H. Committee, which was thereupon dissolved. The East Riding County Council took on responsibility for financing the county V.C.H., with some help from the City of York. That arrangement ended in 1974 under the Act of 1972, which transferred much the greater part of the East Riding to the new county of Humberside, centred on Hull. Councillors

---

[4] Cf. *The Middlesex Victoria County History Council 1955–84* (University of London Institute of Historical Research, 1984).

[5] Camden, Hackney, Hammersmith and Fulham, Isling-ton, Kensington and Chelsea, Tower Hamlets, Westminster.

[6] Barking, Havering, Newham, Redbridge, and Waltham Forest.

and officers of the new county expressed a reluctance to assume the sponsorship of the East Riding V.C.H., but shortly before the old County Council was dissolved the chairman of its finance committee, the late Sir John Dunnington-Jefferson, and the Chief Executive, the late Mr. R. A. Whitley, made an unusual proposal: the East Riding County Council offered an interest-free loan, which was gratefully accepted, to the Institute of Historical Research with the intention that the Institute should use the income from the capital to continue the compilation of the East Riding V.C.H., employing the existing editorial staff or their successors for the purpose, until the loan was repayable to the successor Authorities in the year 2000. Under that arrangement the East Riding V.C.H. is making good progress.

The financial provisions of the V.C.H. vary from county to county. Most recently, a fund has been raised to enable the completion of the Cambridgeshire V.C.H., for which previously the greater part of the work had been done using the Institute's own resources. When those appeared to be inadequate to finish the task, the County Council, several of the Colleges, and some other local benefactors generously contributed towards the cost of employing an editorial assistant. There are thus locally raised funds in each of the twelve counties where the V.C.H. is in progress. In the face of changes and restrictions imposed by central government on local government finance some of those funds look, in 1990, to be less than totally secure.

The expansion mentioned above has increased the full-time staff of the V.C.H. from 29 in 1970 to 34 in 1990. In addition there are a few part-time staff and regular voluntary assistants. Since members of the staff are well qualified and their expertise and experience are an important asset, it is worth noting that 15 of the 34 were on the V.C.H. staff, not all of them in the same capacity, in 1970. Professor R. B. Pugh, who had become General Editor in 1949, presided over the postwar revival of the V.C.H., bringing in new local sponsors to increase the number of counties in progress and the rate of production, enlarging the scope of the volumes and the range of sources used, modernizing the layout, training a growing staff. It is primarily to him that the V.C.H. owes its present character and reputation. He retired in 1977, and died in 1982.[7] He was succeeded by Mr. C. R. Elrington, who had been Deputy Editor since 1968; Dr. C. R. J. Currie became Deputy Editor in 1978. Others who were active in the revival and expansion of the V.C.H. after 1949 and have retired since 1970 are the staff Architect, Mrs. Margaret Tomlinson, and the editors in Wiltshire and Essex, Miss Elizabeth Crittall and Mr. W. R. Powell. The early deaths of two county editors, Mr. A. T. Gaydon of Shropshire in 1974, who had retired on grounds of health in 1970, and Dr. B. E. Harris of Cheshire in 1988, each in his forties, removed two experienced and energetic workers.

All the volumes that have been issued since 1970, as indeed since 1935, have been published for the University of London Institute of Historical Research by Oxford University Press. The number of copies printed of each volume was usually 1,000.[8] The production of the volumes has been committed to various

---

[7] Cf. *The Times*, 6 Dec. 1982; *Bull. Inst. Hist. Res.* lvi. 123–5; *Wilts. Coroners' Bills 1752–96* (Wilts. Rec. Soc. xxxvi), pp. xiii–xvii.

[8] Exceptions were *Essex* vi (1,200) and Bibliography Sup-plement (950), *Mdx.* iv and v (each 1,200), *Salop.* ii (1,200), *Som.* iii (1,200), *Staffs.* xvii (1,300), *Suss.* index (750), *Wilts.* i (2) (1,400).

firms of printers,[9] but nearly three quarters of the volumes that have been published since 1935 were printed by the printing division of Oxford University Press; the closure of the printing works and bindery there in the spring of 1989 was therefore a severe blow to the V.C.H. and a sad break with a tradition of more than half a century.

[9] Robert Maclehose and Co. Ltd. (*Cambs.* v, *Essex* vii, *Glos.* vii, x, and xi, *Mdx.* v, *Salop.* ii and iii, *Staffs.* vi, *Yorks. E.R.* ii), Bigwood & Staple Ltd. (*Mdx.* ix, *Som.* v, *Suss.* vi (2 and 3), *Wilts.* xiii), Alan Sutton Ltd. (*Glos.* iv, *Salop.* xi, *Suss.* index), H. Charlesworth & Co. Ltd. (*Essex* Bibliography Supplement, *Salop.* iv, *Yorks. E.R.* vi), the Pitman Press (*Ches.* iii, *Oxon.* iv), the Alden Press (*Yorks. E.R.* iii), E. J. Brill of Leiden (*Wilts.* viii), and the Scolar Press (*Suss.* vi (1)).

STATE OF THE V.C.H.

(at December 1990)

COUNTIES COMPLETED, IN PROGRESS, DORMANT, AND UNSTARTED

Complete

Bedfordshire	Huntingdonshire	Worcestershire
Berkshire	Lancashire	Yorkshire
Buckinghamshire	Rutland	(general volumes)
Hampshire	Surrey	Yorkshire, North Riding
Hertfordshire	Warwickshire	Yorkshire, City of York

In progress

Cambridgeshire	Middlesex	Staffordshire
Cheshire	Oxfordshire	Sussex
Essex	Shropshire	Wiltshire
Gloucestershire	Somerset	Yorkshire, East Riding

(General volumes complete for Cambridgeshire, Essex, Middlesex, Oxfordshire, Somerset, Staffordshire, Sussex, Wiltshire, Yorkshire)

Dormant

Cornwall	Durham	London
Cumberland	Herefordshire	Norfolk
Derbyshire	Kent	Northamptonshire
Devonshire	Leicestershire	Nottinghamshire
Dorset	Lincolnshire	Suffolk

(General volumes complete for Derbyshire, Durham, Kent, Leicestershire, Nottinghamshire, Suffolk)

Unstarted   Northumberland   Westmorland   Yorkshire, West Riding

Two additional volumes have long been proposed, one on the Six Northern Counties (Cumberland, Durham, Lancashire, Northumberland, Westmorland, and Yorkshire) in the Roman period, the other on London and Middlesex: government, parliamentary representation, industrialization, and urbanization.

COUNTIES IN PROGRESS AND DORMANT:
WORK PUBLISHED, IN PROGRESS, AND TO BE STARTED

(The number following the date of publication is the International Standard Book Number. The absence of such a number shows that in 1990 the book was out of print. The titles of some chapters have been abbreviated.)

Cambridgeshire and the Isle of Ely

Published

I   Natural History, Early Man, Anglo-Saxon Remains, Domesday (1938; 0 7129 0241 4)

II   Ancient Earthworks, Social and Economic History, Population Table, Ecclesiastical History, Religious Houses, Industries, Political History (1948; 0 7129 0242 2)

III   City and University of Cambridge, Colleges and Halls (1959; 0 7129 0243 0)

IV   Isle of Ely: Liberty and City of Ely; Ely, North and South Witchford, and Wisbech hundreds (1953; 0 7129 0244 9)

Index to Volumes I–IV (1960; 0 19 722697 3)

V   Longstowe and Wetherley hundreds [west Cambridgeshire]; Sport; index (1973; 0 19 722717 1)

9

VI Chilford, Radfield, and Whittlesford hundreds [south-east Cambridgeshire]; index (1978; 0 19 722746 5)

VII Roman Cambridgeshire; index (1978; 0 19 722748 1)

VIII Armingford and Thriplow hundreds [south-west Cambridgeshire]; index (1982; 0 19 722757 0)

IX Chesterton, Northstowe, and Papworth hundreds (north and north-west of Cambridge); index (1989; 0 19 722773 2)

In progress

X Cheveley, Flendish, Staine, and Staploe hundreds (east Cambridgeshire)

Cheshire

Published

I Physique, Prehistory, Roman Period, Anglo-Saxon Cheshire, Domesday; index (1987; 0 19 722761 9)

II Administrative History, Parliamentary Representation, Forests, Population Table; index (1979; 0 19 722749 X)

III Church before the Reformation, Diocese of Chester, Roman Catholicism, Protestant Nonconformity, Religious Houses, Chester Cathedral, Education before 1903, Schools; index (1980; 0 19 722754 6)

In progress

V City of Chester

To be started

Economic History, Industries; Broxton, Bucklow, Eddisbury, Macclesfield, Nantwich, Northwich, and Wirral hundreds

Cornwall

Published

I Natural History, Early Man, Anglo-Saxon Remains, Stone Circles, Early Christian Monuments, Ancient Earthworks, Maritime History, Industries (1906; 0 7129 0672 X)

II Romano-British Cornwall, Domesday (1924; two uncased parts re-issued with volume I)

To be started

Ecclesiastical History, Religious Houses, Political History, Social and Economic History, Population Table, Agriculture, Forests, Education, Sport; all topography

Cumberland

Published

I Natural History, Early Man, Pre-Norman Remains, Domesday (1901; 0 7129 0302 X)

II Ecclesiastical History, Religious Houses, Monumental Effigies, Industries, Sport, Forestry (1905; 0 7129 0303 8)

To be started

Anglo-Saxon, Social and Economic History, Population Table, Agriculture, Earthworks, Education, Maritime History; all topography

Derbyshire

Published

I Natural History, Early Man, Romano-British Remains, Anglo-Saxon Remains, Early Christian Art, Domesday, Ancient Earthworks, Forestry (1905)

II Ecclesiastical History, Religious Houses, Political History, Social and Economic History, Population Table, Schools, Sport, Agriculture, Industries (1907; 0 7129 0447 6)

To be started

All topography

Devonshire

Published

I Natural History, Early Man, Anglo-Saxon Remains, Domesday, Feudal Baronage, Ancient Earthworks (1906; 0 7129 0671 1)

To be started

Roman Devonshire, Ecclesiastical History, Religious Houses, Political History, Social and Economic History, Population Table, Industries, Agriculture, Forests, Education, Sport, Maritime History; all topography

Dorset

Published

II Ecclesiastical History, Religious Houses, Political History, Maritime History, Social and Economic History, Population Table, Agriculture, Forestry, Sport, Industries (1908; 0 7129 0670 3)

III Domesday; index to Volumes II and III (1968; 0 19 722718 X)

To be started

Physique, Prehistory, Roman Dorset, Anglo-Saxon; all topography

Durham

Published

I Natural History, Early Man, Anglo-Saxon Remains, Contents of St. Cuthbert's Shrine, Boldon Book, Ancient Earthworks, Schools (1905; 0 7129 0304 6)

II Ecclesiastical History, Religious Houses, Political History, Social and Economic History, Population Table, Industries, Agriculture, Forestry, Sport (1907; 0 7129 0305 4)

III City of Durham, Stockton Ward (1928; 0 7129 0306 2)

To be started

Darlington, Easington, and Washington wards

Essex

Published

I Natural History, Early Man, Ancient Earthworks, Anglo-Saxon Remains, Domesday (1903; 0 7129 0774 2)

II Ecclesiastical History, Religious Houses, Political History, Maritime History, Social and Economic History, Population Table, Industries, Schools, Sport, Forestry (1907; 0 7129 0775 0)

III Roman Essex; index to Volumes I–III (1963; 0 7129 0776 9)

IV Ongar hundred [including Chigwell]; index (1956; 0 7129 0777 7)

V Metropolitan Essex since 1850; Waltham hundred and Becontree hundred [part, including Barking

and Ilford]; index (1966; 0 19 722712 0)

VI Becontree hundred [part, including East and West Ham and Walthamstow]; index (1973; 0 19 722719 8)

VII The Liberty of Havering-atte-Bower [including Romford], Chafford hundred [part]; index (1978; 0 19 722720 1)

VIII Chafford hundred [part, including Brentwood] and Harlow hundred; index (1983; 0 19 722721 X)

Bibliography (1959) and Supplement (1987; 0 19 722770 8)

In progress

IX Colchester borough and liberties

To be started

Barstable, Chelmsford, Clavering, Dengie, Dunmow, Freshwell, Hinckford, Lexden, Rochford, Tendring, Thurstable, Uttlesford, Winstree, and Witham hundreds; Chelmsford and Harwich boroughs; Saffron Walden town

Gloucestershire

Published

II Ecclesiastical History, Religious Houses, Social and Economic History, Population Table, Industries, Agriculture, Forestry, Sport, Schools (1907; 0 7129 0555 3)

IV City of Gloucester; index (1988; 0 19 722771 6)

VI Slaughter hundred [including Stow-on-the-Wold] and Tewkesbury and Westminster hundreds [parts]; index (1965)

VII Brightwells Barrow and Rapsgate hundreds [including Fairford and Lechlade]; index (1981; 0 19 722755 4)

VIII Cleeve, Deerhurst, and Tibblestone hundreds, Tewkesbury and Westminster hundreds [parts], and Tewkesbury borough; index (1968; 0 19 722724 4)

X Westbury and Whitstone hundreds [including Newnham and Stonehouse]; index (1972; 0 19 722725 2)

XI Bisley and Longtree hundreds [including Stroud and Tetbury]; index (1976; 0 19 722745 7)

In progress

I Physique, Prehistory, Roman Gloucestershire, Anglo-Saxon Gloucestershire, Domesday

V The Forest of Dean: Bledisloe and St. Briavels hundreds

To be started

Administrative History, Parliamentary Representation, Communications; Barton Regis, Berkeley, Botloe, Bradley, Cheltenham, Crowthorne and Minety, Dudstone and Kings Barton, Grumbalds Ash, Henbury, Kiftsgate, Duchy of Lancaster, Langley and Swineshead, Pucklechurch, and Thornbury hundreds; City of Bristol, Cirencester borough

Herefordshire

Published

I Natural History, Early Man, Romano-British Herefordshire, Ancient Earthworks, Domesday, Political History, Agriculture (1908; 0 7129 0669 X)

To be started

Anglo-Saxon Antiquities, Ecclesiastical History, Religious Houses, Social and Economic History, Population Table, Industries, Forests, Education, Sport; all topography

Kent

Published

I Natural History, Early Man, Anglo-Saxon Remains, Ancient Earthworks, Agriculture, Forestry, Sport (1908; 0 7129 0606 1)

II Ecclesiastical History, Religious Houses, Maritime History (1926; 0 7129 0607 X)

III Romano-British Remains, Domesday, Political History, Social and Economic History, Population Table, Industries (1932; 0 7129 0608 8)

To be started

Schools; all topography

Leicestershire

Published

I Natural History, Early Man, Romano-British Leicestershire, Anglo-Saxon Remains, Ancient Earthworks, Domesday, Ecclesiastical History (1907)

II Religious Houses, Roman Catholicism, Political History, Agrarian History, Forests (1954)

III Industries, Roads, Canals, Railways, Population, Artists, Education, Sport; index to Volumes I–III (1955; 0 7129 0369 0)

IV City of Leicester; index (1958; 0 7129 1044 1)

V Gartree hundred [including Market Harborough]; index (1964)

To be started

Framland, East and West Goscote, Guthlaxton, and Sparkenhoe hundreds

Lincolnshire

Published

II Ecclesiastical History, Religious Houses, Political History, Social and Economic History, Population Table, Industries, Agriculture, Forestry, Schools, Sport (1906; 0 7129 1045 X)

To be started

Physique, Prehistory, Roman Lincolnshire, Anglo-Saxon Lincolnshire, Domesday, Maritime History; all topography

London

Published

I Romano-British London, Anglo-Saxon Remains, Ecclesiastical History, Religious Houses (1909; 0 7129 0605 3)

To be started

Social and Economic History, Industries, Education; all topography [Population Table included in Middlesex II]

Middlesex

Published

I Physique, Archaeology, Domesday, Ecclesiastical Organization, the Jews, Religious Houses, Educa-

tion, Schools, the University of London; index (1969; 0 19 722713 9)

II Ancient Earthworks, Political History, Social and Economic History, Population Table, Industries, Agriculture, Forestry, Sport; Spelthorne hundred [part, including Hampton] (1911)

III Spelthorne hundred [part, including Staines], Isleworth hundred, Elthorne hundred [part]; index to Volumes II and III (1962; 0 7129 1034 4)

IV Elthorne hundred [part, including Hillingdon with Uxbridge] and Gore hundred [part: Edgware and Harrow]; index (1971; 0 19 722727 9)

V Gore hundred [part, including Hendon] and Edmonton hundred [including Edmonton, Enfield, and Tottenham]; index (1976; 0 19 722742 2)

VI Ossulstone hundred [part, including Finchley and Hornsey]; index (1980; 0 19 722750 3)

VII Ossulstone hundred [part: Acton, Ealing, Chiswick, and Willesden]; index (1982; 0 19 722756 2)

VIII Ossulstone hundred [part]: Islington and Stoke Newington; index (1985; 0 19 722762 7)

IX Ossulstone hundred [part]: Hampstead and Paddington; index (1989; 0 19 722772 4)

In progress

X Ossulstone hundred [part]: Bethnal Green, Hackney, and Stepney

To be started

Ossulstone hundred [the remainder, including Chelsea, Fulham, Hammersmith, Kensington, St. Marylebone, and Westminster]

Norfolk

Published

I Natural History, Early Man, Romano-British Remains, Anglo-Saxon Remains (1901; 0 7129 0645 2)

II Domesday, the Danegeld, Ecclesiastical History, Religious Houses, Political History, Medieval Painting, Early Christian Art (1906; 0 7129 0646 0)

To be started

Social and Economic History, Population Table, Industries, Agriculture, Forests, Maritime History, Ancient Earthworks, Education, Sport; all topography

Northamptonshire

Published

I Natural History, Early Man, Romano-British Remains, Anglo-Saxon Remains, Domesday, Monumental Effigies (1902; 0 7129 0449 2)

II Ecclesiastical History, Religious Houses, Early Christian Art, Schools, Industries, Forestry, Sport, Ancient Earthworks; soke of Peterborough, Willybrook hundred (1906; 0 7129 0450 6)

III Northampton borough, Polebrook, Navisford, and Huxloe hundreds, Higham Ferrers borough (1930; 0 7129 0451 4)

IV Higham Ferrers, Spelhoe, Hamfordshoe, Orlingbury, and Wymersley hundreds (1937; 0 7129 0452 2)

Northamptonshire Families (1906)

To be started

Political History, Social and Economic History, Population Table, Agriculture; Cleley, Corby, Fawsley, Guilsborough, Nobottle Grove, Greens Norton, Rothwell, King's Sutton, Towcester, and Chipping Warden hundreds

Nottinghamshire

Published

I Natural History, Early Man, Anglo-Saxon Remains, Domesday, Ancient Earthworks, Political History, Forestry (1906; 0 7129 0453 0)

II Romano-British Nottinghamshire, Ecclesiastical History, Religious Houses, Schools, Social and Economic History, Population Table, Industries, Agriculture, Sport (1910; 0 7129 0454 9)

To be started

All topography

Oxfordshire

Published

I Natural History, Early Man, Romano-British Remains, Anglo-Saxon Remains, Domesday, Political History, Schools (1939; 0 7129 0456 5)

II Ecclesiastical History, Religious Houses, Social and Economic History, Population Table, Industries, Agriculture, Forestry, Ancient Earthworks, Sport (1907; 0 7129 1041 7)

III University of Oxford, Colleges and Halls; index (1954)

IV City of Oxford; index (1979; 0 19 722714 7)

V Bullingdon hundred [including Cowley and Cuddesdon]; index (1957; 0 7129 1042 5)

VI Ploughley hundred [including Bicester]; index (1959)

VII Dorchester and Thame hundreds; index (1962)

VIII Lewknor and Pirton hundreds [including Watlington]; index (1964)

IX Bloxham hundred [including Adderbury]; index (1969; 0 19 722726 0)

X Banbury hundred; index (1972; 0 19 722728 7)

XI Wootton hundred (northern part) [including Deddington]; index (1983; 0 19 722758 9)

XII Wootton hundred (southern part, including Woodstock); index (1990; 0 19 722774 0)

In progress

XIII Bampton hundred [part]

To be started

Bampton [part], Binfield, Chadlington, Ewelme, and Langtree hundreds

Shropshire

Published

I Natural History, Early Man, Romano-British Shropshire, Domesday, Ancient Earthworks, Industries, Forestry (1908)

II Ecclesiastical Organization, Religious Houses, Schools, Sport, Population Table; index to Volumes I and II (1973; 0 19 722729 5)

III County Government, Parliamentary Representation; index (1979; 0 19 722730 9)

IV Agriculture; index (1989; 0 19 722775 9)

VIII Condover and Ford hundreds [including Alberbury-with-Cardeston and Pontesbury]; index

(1968; 0 19 722731 7)

XI Telford: Wenlock liberty and borough [part, including Madeley] and Bradford hundred [part, including Wellington]; index (1985; 0 19 722763 5)

In progress

V Architecture

X Munslow hundred [part] and remainder of Wenlock liberty and borough

To be started

Brimstree, Chirbury, Clun, Oswestry, Overs, Pimhill, Purslow, and Stottesdon hundreds, remainder of Bradford and Munslow hundreds, Bridgnorth, Ludlow, and Shrewsbury boroughs

Somerset

Published

I Natural History, Early Man, Romano-British Somerset, Anglo-Saxon Remains, Domesday (1906; 0 7129 0375 5)

II Ecclesiastical History, Religious Houses, Political History, Maritime History, Social and Economic History, Population Table, Industries, Schools, Ancient Earthworks, Agriculture, Forestry, Sport; index to Volumes I and II (1911)

III Kingsbury [part], Pitney, Somerton, and Tintinhull hundreds [including Langport, Somerton, and Ilchester]; index (1974; 0 19 722739 2)

IV Crewkerne, Martock, and South Petherton hundreds; index (1978; 0 19 722747 3)

V Whitley [part] and Williton and Freemanors [part, including Watchet and Williton] hundreds; index (1985; 0 19 722764 3)

In progress

VI Andersfield, Cannington, and North Petherton hundreds, Bridgwater borough

To be started

Abdick and Bulstone, Bath Forum, Bempstone, Brent with Wrington, Bruton, Carhampton, Catsash, Chew, Chewton, North Curry, Frome, Glaston Twelve Hides, Hampton and Claverton, Hartcliffe with Bedminster, Horethorne, Houndsborough, Barwick and Coker, Keynsham, Kilmersdon, Kingsbury [remainder], Milverton, Norton Ferris, Portbury, Stone, Taunton and Taunton Deane, Wellow, Wells Forum, Whitley [remainder], Whitstone, Williton and Freemanors [remainder], and Winterstoke hundreds, Bath city, Taunton borough, and Mells and Leigh liberty

Staffordshire

Published

I Natural History, Early Man, Romano-British Staffordshire, Anglo-Saxon Remains, Political History, Social and Economic History, Population Table, Ancient Earthworks (1908; 0 7129 0308 9)

II Industries, Roads, Canals, Railways, Forests, Sport; index to Volumes I and II (1967; 0 19 722715 5)

III Ecclesiastical Organization, Roman Catholicism, Protestant Nonconformity, Religious Houses; index (1970; 0 19 722732 5)

IV Domesday; West Cuttlestone hundred; index (1958; 0 7129 1038 7)

V East Cuttlestone hundred [including Cannock and Rugeley]; index (1959; 0 7129 1039 5)

VI Agriculture, Schools, Keele university; Stafford borough; index (1979; 0 19 722733 3)

VIII Newcastle-under-Lyme borough, the City of Stoke-on-Trent [part of Pirehill hundred]; index (1963)

XVII Offlow hundred [part: West Bromwich, Smethwick, Walsall]; index (1976; 0 19 722743 0)

XX Seisdon hundred [part, including Amblecote and Tettenhall]; index (1984; 0 19 722765 1)

XIV City of Lichfield; index (1990; 0 19 722778 3)

In progress

XI Leek and the Moorlands: Totmonslow hundred [part]

To be started

Remainder of Offlow, Pirehill, Seisdon, and Totmonslow hundreds

Suffolk

Published

I Natural History, Early Man, Romano-British Suffolk, Anglo-Saxon Remains, Domesday, Ancient Earthworks, Social and Economic History, Population Table (1911; 0 7129 0647 9)

II Ecclesiastical History, Religious Houses, Political History, Maritime History, Industries, Schools, Sport, Agriculture, Forestry (1907; 0 7129 0648 7)

To be started

All topography

Sussex

Published

I Natural History, Early Man, Anglo-Saxon Remains, Domesday, Ancient Earthworks, Political History (1905; 0 7129 0585 5)

II Ecclesiastical History, Religious Houses, Maritime History, Social and Economic History, Population Table, Industries, Agriculture, Forestry, Architecture, Schools, Sport (1907; 0 7129 0586 3)

III Romano-British Sussex; the City of Chichester (1935; 0 7129 0587 1)

IV Chichester rape (1953; 0 7129 0588 X)

VI (1) Bramber rape (southern part) [including Shoreham and Worthing]; index (1980; 0 19 722753 8)

VI (2) Bramber rape (north-western part) including Horsham; index (1986; 0 19 722767 8)

VI (3) Bramber rape (north-eastern part) including Crawley New Town; index (1987; 0 19 722768 6)

VII Lewes rape [including Brighton, Hove, and Lewes boroughs (1940; 0 7129 0589 8)

IX Hastings rape [including Hastings, Rye, and Winchelsea boroughs (1937; 0 7129 0590 1)

Index to Volumes I–IV, VII, and IX (1984; 0 19 722766 X)

In progress

V (1) Arundel rape (south-western part) including Arundel

V (2) Arundel rape (south-eastern part) including Littlehampton

To be started
Remainder of Arundel rape; Pevensey rape

Wiltshire

Published

I (1) Physique, Archaeological Gazetteer (1957)

I (2) Prehistoric Archaeology, Roman Period, Pagan Saxon Period; index to parts 1 and 2 (1973; 0 19 722735 X)

II Anglo-Saxon Wiltshire, Anglo-Saxon Art, Domesday; index (1955; 0 7129 1047 6)

III Ecclesiastical History, Roman Catholicism, Protestant Nonconformity, Religious Houses; index (1956; 0 7129 1048 4)

IV Economic History, Industries, Roads, Canals, Railways, Population Table, Sport, Spas and Mineral Springs, Freemasonry, Forests; index (1959)

V County Government, Feudal Wiltshire, Parliamentary History, Public Health, Education; index (1957)

VI Wilton borough, Old Salisbury borough, City of New Salisbury, Underditch hundred; index (1962; 0 7129 1032 8)

VII Bradford, Melksham, and Potterne and Cannings hundreds [including Bradford-on-Avon, Melksham, and Trowbridge]; index (1953; 0 7129 1036 0)

VIII Warminster, Westbury, and Whorwellsdown hundreds; index (1965; 0 19 722710 4)

IX Kingsbridge hundred [including Swindon and Wootton Bassett]; index (1970; 0 19 722736 8)

X Swanborough hundred [including Market Lavington], Devizes borough; index (1975; 0 19 722740 6)

XI Downton and Elstub and Everleigh hundreds [including Downton, East Knoyle with Hindon, and Wroughton]; index (1980; 0 19 722751 1)

XII Ramsbury and Selkley hundreds [including Ramsbury, Avebury, and Preshute], Marlborough borough; index (1983; 0 19 722759 7)

XIII South-west Wiltshire: Chalke and Dunworth hundreds [including Tisbury]; index (1987; 0 19 722769 7)

In progress

XIV Malmesbury hundred and borough

XV Amesbury and Branch and Dole hundreds

To be started

Alderbury, Calne, Cawdon and Cadworth, Chippenham, North and South Damerham, Frustfield, Heytesbury, Highworth, Cricklade, and Staple, Kinwardstone, and Mere hundreds

Yorkshire, East Riding

Published

I The City of Kingston upon Hull; index (1969)

II Dickering wapentake [including Bridlington and Filey]; index (1974; 0 19 722738 4)

III Ouse and Derwent wapentake [including Hemingbrough] and Harthill wapentake [part]; index (1976; 0 19 722744 9)

IV Harthill wapentake [part, including North and South Cave and Cottingham]; index (1979; 0 19 722752 X)

V Holderness wapentake, southern part [including Hedon, Patrington, and Withernsea]; index (1984; 0 19 722760 0)

VI Beverley borough and liberties; index (1989; 0 19 722776 7)

In progress

VII Holderness wapentake, northern part [including Hornsea]

To be started

Buckrose, Howdenshire, and Harthill (remainder) wapentakes

LISTS OF CONTENTS

BELOW are reprinted the lists of contents of all the volumes of the *History* published since 1970, excluding the *General Introduction*, its Supplement, and the Sussex Index volume. An abbreviated form of the contents pages for the Essex Bibliography Supplement is included here. A few changes have been made either to correct errors that have been discovered in the orginal lists or to remove minor inconsistencies. No attempt has been made to achieve uniformity.

CAMBRIDGESHIRE AND THE ISLE OF ELY

VOLUME FIVE

Edited by C. R. Elrington

(1973)

		PAGE
Dedication	.	v
Contents	.	ix
List of Illustrations	.	xi
List of Maps	.	xii
Editorial Note	.	xiii
Classes of Documents in the Public Record Office used	.	xiv
Note of Abbreviations	.	xv
Topography	Architectural descriptions by MARGARET TOMLINSON and A. P. BAGGS; sections on nonconformity, education, and charities drafted by DIANE K. BOLTON (Longstowe hundred) and A. M. ROWLAND (Wetherley hundred)	
Longstowe Hundred	By R. W. DUNNING and A. P. M. WRIGHT	1
Bourn	By DIANE K. BOLTON	4
Caldecote	By DIANE K. BOLTON	16
Caxton	By R. W. DUNNING	26
Croxton	By W. B. STEPHENS	36
Eltisley	By the late G. R. DUNCOMBE	46
Great and Little Eversden	By CELIA B. CLARKE and C. R. ELRINGTON	59
Gamlingay	By R. W. DUNNING	68
Little Gransden	By A. P. M. WRIGHT	87
Hardwick	By the late G. R. DUNCOMBE	99
Hatley St. George	By the late G. R. DUNCOMBE	104
Kingston	By the late G. R. DUNCOMBE	111
Longstowe	By R. W. DUNNING	120
Toft	By the late G. R. DUNCOMBE	127
Wetherley Hundred	By A. P. M. WRIGHT	137
Arrington	By the late G. R. DUNCOMBE and JENNIFER I. KERMODE	140
Barrington	By A. P. M. WRIGHT	147
Barton	By A. P. M. WRIGHT	160
Comberton	By A. P. M. WRIGHT	175
Coton	By A. P. M. WRIGHT	189
Grantchester	By A. P. M. WRIGHT	198
Harlton	By A. M. ROWLAND	214
Haslingfield	By A. P. M. WRIGHT	227

PAGE

Orwell . . . . . . By Jennifer I. Kermode . . . 241
Shepreth . . . . . By Jennifer I. Kermode . . . 251
Wimpole . . . . . By Jennifer I. Kermode . . . 263
Analysis of Hearth Tax Assessments, Longstowe and
   Wetherley Hundreds . . . . By C. A. F. Meekings . . . 273
Sport
  Horse-racing . . . . . By A. P. M. Wright . . . 279
  Rowing . . . . . . By the late Frederick Brittain and
                                    A. M. Rowland . . . 287
  Football . . . . . . By the late G. R. Duncombe . . 291
  Cricket . . . . . . By the late G. R. Duncombe . . 294
  Fox-hunting . . . . . By R. W. Dunning . . . 296
  Fishing . . . . . . By the late G. R. Duncombe . . 297
  Wildfowling and Shooting . . . By R. W. Dunning . . . 299
  Skating . . . . . . By R. W. Dunning . . . 302
Index . . . . . . By A. P. M. Wright . . . 304
Corrigenda to Volumes I–IV 337

VOLUME SIX
Edited by A. P. M. Wright
(1978)

PAGE

Dedication v
Contents ix
List of Illustrations xi
List of Maps xiii
Editorial Note xv
Classes of Documents in the Public Record Office used xvii
Note on Abbreviations xix
Topography . . . . . Architectural descriptions by A. P. Baggs
  Chilford Hundred . . . . By A. P. M. Wright . . . 1
    Great and Little Abington . . . By A. P. M. Wright . . . 3
    Babraham . . . . . By Adrienne B. Rosen . . . 19
    Bartlow . . . . . By Adrienne B. Rosen . . . 30
    Castle Camps . . . . . By A. P. M. Wright . . . 36
    Shudy Camps . . . . . By A. P. M. Wright . . . 49
    Hildersham . . . . . By A. P. M. Wright . . . 59
    Horseheath . . . . . By Adrienne B. Rosen and A. P. M.
                                   Wright 70
    Linton . . . . . . By A. P. M. Wright . . . 80
    Pampisford . . . . . By Adrienne B. Rosen . . . 105
    West Wickham . . . . . By A. P. M. Wright . . . 113
  Radfield Hundred . . . . By Susan M. Keeling . . . 125
    Balsham . . . . . By Susan M. Keeling . . . 127
    Brinkley . . . . . By Susan M. Keeling . . . 136
    Burrough Green . . . . By Susan M. Keeling . . . 141
    Carlton cum Willingham . . . By A. P. M. Wright . . . 148
    Dullingham . . . . . By A. P. M. Wright . . . 157
    Stetchworth . . . . . By Susan M. Keeling . . . 170
    Westley Waterless . . . . By Susan M. Keeling . . . 177
    Weston Colville . . . . By A. P. M. Wright . . . 182
    West Wratting . . . . By Susan M. Keeling . . . 191
  Whittlesford Hundred . . . . By A. P. M. Wright . . . 199
    Duxford . . . . . By A. P. M. Wright . . . 201
    Hinxton . . . . . By Adrienne B. Rosen . . . 220

		PAGE
Ickleton	By Adrienne B. Rosen	230
Sawston	By Adrienne B. Rosen	246
Whittlesford	By A. P. M. Wright	263
Analysis of Hearth Tax Assessments, Chilford, Radfield, and Whittlesford Hundreds	By the late C. A. F. Meekings	277
Index	By Susan M. Keeling	283
Corrigenda to Volumes II, IV, and V		314

VOLUME SEVEN
Roman Cambridgeshire
Edited by J. J. Wilkes and C. R. Elrington
(1978)

		PAGE
Dedication		v
Contents		ix
List of Illustrations		xi
List of Maps		xiii
Editorial Note		xv
Note on Abbreviations		xvi
Roman Cambridgeshire	By D. M. Browne	
Historical Survey		1
Appendices: Place-names; Military Remains; Dykes		4
The Physical Environment		6
Roads		15
Appendix: Milestones and Other Inscriptions		28
Settlements		29
Agriculture		59
Appendix: Salt Production		61
Currency		61
Material Culture		65
Religion and Burial		84
Index	By Susan M. Keeling	93

VOLUME EIGHT
Armingford and Thriplow Hundreds
Edited by A. P. M. Wright
(1982)

		PAGE
Dedication		v
Contents		ix
List of Illustrations		xi
List of Maps and Plans		xii
Editorial Note		xiii
Classes of Documents in the Public Record Office used		xiv
Note on Abbreviations		xv
Topography	Architectural descriptions compiled or revised by A. P. Baggs	
Armingford Hundred	By A. P. M. Wright	1
Abington Pigotts	By A. P. M. Wright	4
Bassingbourn	By A. P. M. Wright	12
Croydon cum Clopton	By A. P. M. Wright	30
East Hatley	By A. P. M. Wright	43
Kneesworth	By A. P. M. Wright	49
Litlington	By A. P. M. Wright	54

PAGE

Melbourn	By S. M. Keeling		67
Meldreth	By S. M. Keeling		83
Guilden Morden	By A. P. M. Wright		97
Steeple Morden	By A. P. M. Wright		111
Shingay	By S. M. Keeling		124
Tadlow	By A. P. M. Wright		127
Wendy	By S. M. Keeling		135
Whaddon	By S. M. Keeling		142
Thriplow Hundred	By A. P. M. Wright		152
Fowlmere	By S. M. Keeling		155
Foxton	By A. P. M. Wright		165
Harston	By A. P. M. Wright		178
Hauxton and Newton	By A. P. M. Wright		194
Great Shelford	By S. M. Keeling		207
Little Shelford	By S. M. Keeling		220
Stapleford	By A. P. M. Wright		227
Thriplow	By S. M. Keeling		238
Trumpington	By A. P. M. Wright		248
Analysis of Hearth Tax Assessments, Armingford and Thriplow Hundreds	By the late C. A. F. Meekings		268
Index	By S. M. Keeling		273
Corrigenda to Volumes I, V, and VI			301

VOLUME NINE

Chesterton, Northstowe, and Papworth Hundreds
(North and North-West of Cambridge)
Edited by A. P. M. Wright and C. P. Lewis
(1989)

PAGE

Dedication		v
Contents		ix
List of Illustrations		x
List of Maps and Plans		xii
Editorial Note		xiii
Contributors to the Cambridgeshire V.C.H. fund		xiii
Classes of Documents in the Public Record Office used		xiv
Note on Abbreviations		xvi
Topography	Architectural descriptions compiled or revised by A. P. Baggs	
Introduction	By A. P. M. Wright	1
Chesterton Hundred	By A. P. M. Wright	3
Chesterton	By A. P. M. Wright	5
Childerley	By A. P. M. Wright	39
Cottenham	By C. P. Lewis	48
Dry Drayton	By A. P. M. Wright	71
Histon	By C. P. Lewis	90
Westwick	By C. P. Lewis	107
Northstowe Hundred	By A. P. M. Wright	113
Girton	By A. P. M. Wright	115
Impington	By C. P. Lewis	129
Landbeach	By A. P. M. Wright	138
Lolworth	By A. P. M. Wright	156
Madingley	By A. P. M. Wright	165
Milton	By A. P. M. Wright	177
Oakington	By A. P. M. Wright	192

PAGE

Rampton . . . . . By C. P. Lewis 211
Long Stanton . . . . . By C. P. Lewis 220
Waterbeach . . . . . By A. P. M. Wright . . . 237
Papworth Hundred . . . . By A. P. M. Wright . . . 267
  Boxworth . . . . . By A. P. M. Wright . . . 269
  Conington . . . . . By A. P. M. Wright . . . 280
  Fen Drayton . . . . By A. P. M. Wright . . . 289
  Elsworth . . . . . By A. P. M. Wright . . . 305
  Graveley . . . . . By A. P. M. Wright . . . 320
  Knapwell . . . . . By A. P. M. Wright . . . 332
  Over . . . . . By C. P. Lewis 339
  Papworth Everard . . . By A. P. M. Wright . . . 357
  Papworth St. Agnes . . . By A. P. M. Wright . . . 367
  Swavesey . . . . By C. R. J. Currie . . 374
  Willingham . . . . By C. P. Lewis . . . 398
Analysis of Hearth Tax Assessments, Chesterton,
Northstowe, and Papworth Hundreds . . By the late C. A. F. Meekings . 415
Index 421
Corrigenda to Volumes II–VIII and Index to Volumes I–IV 452

CHESHIRE

VOLUME ONE

Physique, Prehistory, Roman, Anglo-Saxon, and Domesday

Edited by B. E. Harris, assisted by A. T. Thacker

(1987)

PAGE

Dedication v
Contents ix
List of Plates xi
List of Maps, Plans, and Drawings xiii
Editorial Note xv
Note of Abbreviations xvi
Physique . . . . . By Sheila M. Hebblethwaite . . 1
  Geology 4
    Solid Rock Formations 5
    Drift Geology 19
  The Conditions of Settlement 26
Prehistory . . . . . By D. M. T. Longley . . 36
  Hunters and Gatherers 36
  Early Agriculturalists 40
  The First Metalworkers 56
  The Later Bronze Age 92
  Later Prehistory 103
The Roman Period . . . . By D. F. Petch . . . 115
  The Roman Occupation 115
  Chester 117
    The Legionary Fortress 117
    The Status of Roman Chester 164
    The Extra-Mural Area 165
    Deva: Civil Settlement 168
  Settlements outside Chester 187
  Communications 215
  Industries 222

PAGE

Gazetteer 228
Anglo-Saxon Cheshire . . . By A. T. THACKER . . . 237
  Sub-Roman Cheshire 238
  Early Anglo-Saxon Cheshire 243
  Cheshire and North-East Wales under the Mercian Kings 247
  The Impact of the Scandinavians 248
  Scandinavian Settlement 254
  Late Anglo-Saxon Cheshire 260
  Early Estate Organization and the Hundred 263
  The Church in Cheshire 268
  Buildings, Art, and Artefacts 273
  Gazetteer 286
The Cheshire Domesday
  Introduction . . . . . By P. H. SAWYER and A. T. THACKER . 293
    Compilation 293
    Assessments 297
    Tenants 302
    The Boroughs 325
    The Salt-Wiches 328
    The Rural Population 330
    Settlement and the Agrarian Economy 333
  Translation of the Text . . . . By P. H. SAWYER . . . 342
General Index . . . . . By B. E. HARRIS . . . 371
Index of Persons and Places mentioned in Domesday By A. T. THACKER . . . 386

VOLUME TWO
Edited by B. E. Harris
(1979)

PAGE

Dedication v
Contents ix
List of Illustrations xi
List of Maps xii
Editorial Note xiii
Classes of Documents in the Public Record Office, the Cheshire Record Office,
    and the Chester City Record Office xv
Analysis of Cheshire Material in the Deputy Keepers' Reports xvi
Note on Abbreviations xvi
Administrative History . . . By B. E. HARRIS
  The Earldom of Chester 1
  The Palatinate 1301–1547 9
  Palatine Institutions and County Government 1547–1660 36
  The Palatinate 1660–1830 56
  County Government 1660–1830 61
  New Local Authorities 75
  The County Council 1889–1974 82
Parliamentary Representation . . . By J. S. MORRILL . . . 98
  The County Seats 1543–1660 101
  The City of Chester 1543–1660 110
  The County Seats 1660–1832 114
  The City of Chester 1660–1832 127
  Electoral Geography 1832–1974 138
  Cheshire Politics 1832–1974 144
  Tables 162
Forests . . . . . By JUDITH A. GREEN . . 167

PAGE

Table of Population . . . . By Judith A. Green and S. J. Lander . 188

Index . . . . . . By B. E. Harris 250

VOLUME THREE
Edited by B. E. Harris
(1980)

PAGE

Dedication v

Contents ix

List of Illustrations xi

List of Maps and Plans xii

Editorial Note xiii

Classes of Documents in the Public Record Office, the Cheshire Record Office,

    and the Chester City Record Office xiv

Note on Abbreviations xvi

The Church before the Reformation . . . By S. J. Lander 1

The Diocese of Chester . . . . To 1660 by S. J. Lander; from 1660 by

                              A. T. Thacker

    1540–1660 12

    1660–1726 36

    1726–1828 49

    1828–1919 63

    1919–79 78

Roman Catholicism . . . . By S. J. Lander 88

Protestant Nonconformity . . . . By S. J. Lander 101

Religious Houses . . . . . By Ann J. Kettle ; architectural

                              descriptions by A. P. Baggs . 124

  Houses of Benedictine Monks

    The Priory of Birkenhead 128

    The Abbey of Chester 132

  House of Benedictine Nuns

    The Priory of Chester 146

  Houses of Cistercian Monks

    The Abbey of Combermere 150

    The Abbey of Vale Royal 156

  House of Augustinian Canons

    The Abbey of Norton 165

  House of Premonstratensian Canons

    The Priory of Warburton 171

  Friaries

    The Franciscan Friars of Chester 171

    The Dominican Friars of Chester 174

    The Carmelite Friars of Chester 176

    The Friars of the Sack 178

  Hospitals

    The Hospital of St. Giles, Chester 178

    The Hospital of St. John the Baptist, Chester 180

    The Hospital of St. Ursula, Chester 183

    The Hospital of St. Andrew, Denhall 184

    The Hospital of St. Lawrence, Nantwich 186

    The Hospital of St. Nicholas, Nantwich 186

Chester Cathedral . . . . . By B. E. Harris . . . 188

Education before 1903 . . . . By David Wardle . . . 196

Schools . . . . . . By A. T. Thacker . . . 223

  Acton Grammar School 223

  Audlem Grammar School 224

PAGE

Birkenhead School 226
Bunbury Grammar School 227
Calday Grange Grammar School, West Kirby 229
The King's School, Chester 230
The Queen's School 232
Knutsford Grammar School 234
Lymm Grammar School 235
Macclesfield Grammar 237
Malpas Grammar School 240
Mottram in Longendale Grammar School 242
Nantwich Grammar School 243
Sir John Deane's Grammar School, Northwich 244
Sandbach School 247
Stockport Grammar School 249
Wallasey Grammar School 252
Index . . . . . . By A. T. Thacker . . . 255

ESSEX

VOLUME SIX

Edited by W. R. Powell

(1973)

PAGE

Dedication v
Contents ix
List of Illustrations xi
List of Maps and Plans xiii
Editorial Note xv
Essex Victoria County History Committee xvi
Classes of Documents in the Public Record Office used xvii
Classes of Documents in the Essex Record Office used xviii
Note on Abbreviations xix
Topography . . . . . Architectural descriptions based partly on
information from the Department of the
Environment, and revised by Margaret
Tomlinson. Education (except in West
Ham) based on drafts by A. F. J. Brown

Becontree Hundred (continued from Volume V)
East Ham . . . . . By W. R. Powell 1
West Ham . . . . . By W. R. Powell. Modern Churches,
Roman Catholicism, Protestant
Nonconformity, and Judaism by
Avril H. Powell and A. D. Atienza.
Education by W. Simms. Modern
Industries based on a survey by
F. Sainsbury, b.e.m. . . . 43
Little Ilford . . . . . By W. R. Powell 163
Leyton . . . . . . By Hilda E. P. Grieve, b.e.m. Manors and
Ancient Church by Nancy Briggs.
Modern Churches, Roman Catholicism,
Protestant Nonconformity, and Judaism
by Mary L. Savell. Charities by Anne
V. Worsley 174
Walthamstow . . . . . By the late P. H. Reaney, litt.d., and
Hilda E. P. Grieve, b.e.m. Education
and Charities revised by Beryl Board . 240

PAGE

Wanstead . . . . . By Margaret Parsons. Revised by W. R.
Powell 317
Woodford . . . . . By the late Revd. Canon J. L. Fisher and
D. J. Johnson. Charities by Anne V.
Worsley 338
Index . . . . . . By Beryl Board assisted by Susan Liddell 361
Corrigenda to previously published volumes 389

VOLUME SEVEN
Edited by W. R. Powell
(1978)

PAGE

Dedication v
Contents ix
List of Illustrations x
List of Maps and Plans xii
Editorial Note xiii
Essex Victoria County History Committee xiv
Classes of Documents in the Public Record Office used xv
Classes of Documents in the Essex Record Office used xvii
Note on Abbreviations xviii
Topography . . . . . Architectural descriptions prepared in
consultation with A. P. Baggs.
Education and Charities by Beryl A.
Board. Modern Anglican Churches,
Roman Catholicism, Protestant
Nonconformity, and Judaism by
Hilda E. P. Grieve, B.E.M.

The Liberty of Havering-atte-Bower . . By Gladys A. Ward . . . 1
Havering-atte-Bower . . . . By W. R. Powell. Local Government by
Gladys A. Ward . . . 9
Hornchurch . . . . . By W. R. Powell. Local Government by
Gladys A. Ward . . . 25
Romford . . . . . By W. R. Powell 56
Chafford Hundred . . . . By Gladys A. Ward . . . 99
Cranham . . . . . By Gladys A. Ward and D. R. Ransome . 103
North Ockendon . . . . By Gladys A. Ward and D. R. Ransome . 110
South Ockendon . . . . By Gladys A. Ward and D. R. Ransome . 117
Rainham . . . . . By D. R. Ransome . . . 126
Upminster . . . . . By D. R. Ransome . . . 143
Great Warley . . . . . By Joan Hasler and D. R. Ransome . 163
Little Warley . . . . . By Joan Hasler and D. R. Ransome . 174
Wennington . . . . . By Hilda E. P. Grieve, B.E.M. . . 180
Index . . . . . . By Beryl A. Board . . . 191

VOLUME EIGHT
Edited by W. R. Powell, assisted by Beryl A. Board and Norma Knight
(1983)

PAGE

Dedication v
Contents ix
List of Plates xi
List of Maps and Coats of Arms xiii
Editorial Note xv

CONTENTS OF VOLUMES: ESSEX VIII

		PAGE
Essex Victoria County History Committee		xvi
Classes of Documents in the Public Record Office used		xvii
Classes of Documents in the Essex Record Office used		xix
Note on Abbreviations		xxi
Topography	Architectural descriptions prepared in consultation with A. P. BAGGS. Education and Charities by BERYL A. BOARD. Modern Anglican Churches, Roman Catholicism, and Protestant Nonconformity for Chafford Hundred parishes by HILDA E. P. GRIEVE, B.E.M. Revision of Harlow Hundred parishes by W. R. POWELL, BERYL A. BOARD, and NORMA KNIGHT	
Chafford Hundred		
Aveley	By W. R. POWELL and NORMA KNIGHT. Belhus architecture by NANCY BRIGGS	1
Childerditch	By JOAN HASLER and W. R. POWELL. Local Government by BERYL A. BOARD	17
Stifford	By W. R. POWELL	24
Grays Thurrock	By W. R. POWELL	35
West Thurrock	By W. R. POWELL and NORMA KNIGHT	57
South Weald and Brentwood	By GLADYS A. WARD	74
South Weald		74
Brentwood		90
Harlow Hundred	By BERYL A. BOARD	110
Great Hallingbury	By MARGARET PARSONS	113
Little Hallingbury	By MARGARET PARSONS	124
Harlow		131
Harlow Ancient Parish	By the late Revd. Canon J. L. FISHER and VANESSA A. HARDING	131
Harlow Town	By NORMA KNIGHT	149
Hatfield Broad Oak	By MARGARET PARSONS	158
Latton	By the late Revd. Canon J. L. FISHER and VANESSA A. HARDING	186
Matching	By MARGARET PARSONS	196
Netteswell	By the late Revd. Canon J. L. FISHER and VANESSA A. HARDING	206
Great Parndon	By the late Revd. Canon J. L. FISHER and VANESSA A. HARDING	213
Little Parndon	By the late Revd. Canon J. L. FISHER and VANESSA A. HARDING	223
Roydon	By the late Revd. Canon J. L. FISHER and BERYL A. BOARD	227
Sheering	By MARGARET PARSONS	240
Index	By BERYL A. BOARD	251

BIBLIOGRAPHY: SUPPLEMENT

Edited by W. R. Powell, assisted by Beryl A. Board and Shirley Durgan;
compiled by Frank Sainsbury
(1987)

	PAGE
Dedication	v
Contents	ix
Essex V.C.H. Committee	xvi
Editorial Note	xvii

	PAGE
Note on Abbreviations	xx
List of Periodicals Searched	xxiii
Periodicals: Dates and Volume Numbers	xxiv
Essex Bibliography Supplement	
Part I: The County	1
Part II: Biography and Family History	55
Part III: Individual Places and Regions	87
Indexes By Beryl A. Board	
Authors	222
Miscellaneous	242
Articles on Voluntary and Rate-Supported Libraries in *V.C.H. Essex*, Bibliography (1959)	246
Corrigenda to *V.C.H. Essex*, Bibliography (1959)	248

GLOUCESTERSHIRE

VOLUME FOUR
The City of Gloucester
Edited by N. M. Herbert
(1988)

	PAGE
Dedication	v
Contents	ix
List of Plates	xi
List of Maps, Plans, and Other Text Figures	xiii
Editorial Note	xv
Classes of Documents in the Public Record Office used	xvi
Gloucestershire Record Office Accumulations	xvii
Note on Abbreviations	xix
Topography Architectural accounts compiled or revised by A. P. Baggs	
The City of Gloucester	
Introduction By N. M. Herbert	1
Anglo-Saxon Gloucester, *c.* 680 to 1066 By Carolyn Heighway	5
Medieval Gloucester, 1066–1547 By N. M. Herbert	13
Gloucester 1066–1327	13
The Crown and the Borough; Military History	18
Trade and Industry 1066–1327	22
The Achievement of Liberties	28
Town Government 1200–1483	31
Gloucester in the Late Middle Ages	35
Trade and Industry 1327–1547	41
Town Government 1483–1547	54
The Regulation of Trade and Industry	57
The Town and the Religious Communities	59
Topography	63
Early Modern Gloucester, 1547–1720 By Peter Clark	73
Gloucester 1547–1640	73
Population	73
Economic Development	75
Social Structure	81
City Government and Politics	84
Religious and Cultural Life	89

CONTENTS OF VOLUMES: GLOS. IV

PAGE

Gloucester 1640–60 92
  The City and the English Revolution 92
  Population 95
  Economic Development 96
  Social Problems 97
  City Government and Politics 98
  Religious and Cultural Life 100
Gloucester 1660–1720 101
  Population 102
  Economic Development 103
  Social Structure 110
  City Government and Politics 112
  Religious and Cultural Life 117
Topography 1547–1720 120
Gloucester, 1720–1835 . . . By N. M. Herbert . . 124
  Economic Development 1720–91 124
  Economic Development 1791–1835 135
  City Government 141
  Parliamentary Representation 152
  Social and Cultural Life 154
  Topography 159
Gloucester, 1835–1985 . . . By A. R. J. Jurica . . 170
  Economic Development 1835–1914 171
  Economic Development 1914–85 183
  City Government 191
  Parliamentary Representation 205
  Social and Cultural Life 209
  Topography 221
Bridges, Gates, and Walls . . . By N. M. Herbert . . 242
Gloucester Castle . . . By N. M. Herbert . . 245
Public Buildings . . . By N. M. Herbert . . 248
Quay and Docks . . . By A. R. J. Jurica . . 251
Markets and Fairs . . . By N. M. Herbert . . 259
Public Services . . . By N. M. Herbert . . 262
Hospitals . . . By A. R. J. Jurica . . 269
Gloucester Cathedral and the Close . . By N. M. Herbert . . 275
Sites and Remains of Religious Houses . . By N. M. Herbert; St. Oswald's priory by
      Carolyn Heighway . . . 288
Churches and Chapels . . . By A. R. J. Jurica . . 292
Roman Catholicism . . . By A. R. J. Jurica . . 317
Protestant Nonconformity . . . By A. R. J. Jurica . . 319
Other Religious Bodies . . . By A. R. J. Jurica . . 335
Education . . . By N. M. Herbert . . 335
Charities for the Poor . . . By N. M. Herbert . . 351
List of Street Names . . . By N. M. Herbert . . 364
Arms, Seals, Insignia, and Plate . . By A. R. J. Jurica . . 368
List of Bailiffs, 1200–1483 . . . By N. M. Herbert . . 371
List of Aldermen, 1483–1835 . . . By N. M. Herbert . . 374
Outlying Hamlets . . . By A. R. J. Jurica . . 382
Barnwood . . . By A. R. J. Jurica . . 410
Hempsted . . . By N. M. Herbert . . 420
Hucclecote . . . By A. R. J. Jurica . . 430
Matson . . . By A. R. J. Jurica . . 438
Index . . . By N. M. Herbert . . 449

VOLUME SEVEN
Brightwells Barrow and Rapsgate Hundreds
Edited by N. M. Herbert
(1981)

	PAGE
Dedication	v
Contents	ix
List of Illustrations	x
List of Maps	xii
Editorial Note	xiii
Classes of Documents in the Public Record Office used	xv
Gloucestershire Record Office Accumulations	xvi
Note on Abbreviations	xvii

Topography — Architectural descriptions compiled or revised by A. P. BAGGS

		PAGE
Brightwells Barrow Hundred	By A. R. J. JURICA	1
Aldsworth	By A. R. J. JURICA	5
Barnsley	By N. M. HERBERT	13
Bibury	By A. R. J. JURICA	21
Coln St. Aldwyns	By A. R. J. JURICA	44
Eastleach Martin	By N. M. HERBERT	55
Eastleach Turville	By N. M. HERBERT	61
Fairford	By A. R. J. JURICA	69
Hatherop	By A. R. J. JURICA	86
Kempsford	By N. M. HERBERT	96
Lechlade	By N. M. HERBERT	106
Quenington	By A. R. J. JURICA	121
Southrop	By N. M. HERBERT	129
Rapsgate Hundred	By N. M. HERBERT	137
Brimpsfield	By A. R. J. JURICA	140
North Cerney	By N. M. HERBERT	150
Chedworth	By N. M. HERBERT	163
Coberley	By A. R. J. JURICA	174
Colesbourne	By A. R. J. JURICA	183
Cowley	By A. R. J. JURICA	192
Cranham	By A. R. J. JURICA	199
Elkstone	By N. M. HERBERT	210
Rendcomb	By N. M. HERBERT	218
Syde	By N. M. HERBERT	227
Index		233

VOLUME TEN
Edited by C. R. Elrington and N. M. Herbert
(1972)

	PAGE
Dedication	v
Contents	ix
List of Illustrations	xi
List of Maps and Plans	xiii
Editorial Note	xv
Classes of Documents in the Public Record Office used	xvii
Gloucestershire Record Office Accumulations	xix
Note on Abbreviations	xxi

Topography — Architectural descriptions compiled or revised by MARGARET TOMLINSON

PAGE

Westbury Hundred	By BRIAN S. SMITH	1
Blaisdon	By N. M. HERBERT	6
Churcham	By N. M. HERBERT	11
Newnham	By C. R. ELRINGTON	29
Tidenham, including Lancaut	By N. M. HERBERT	50
Westbury-on-Severn	By N. M. HERBERT	79
Woolaston	By BRIAN S. SMITH	102
Whitstone Hundred	By N. M. HERBERT	119
Eastington	By N. M. HERBERT	123
Frampton on Severn	By C. R. ELRINGTON	139
Fretherne and Saul	By C. R. ELRINGTON	155
Frocester	By N. M. HERBERT	170
Hardwicke	By C. R. ELRINGTON	178
Haresfield	By N. M. HERBERT	188
Longney	By C. R. ELRINGTON	197
Moreton Valence	By C. R. ELRINGTON	205
Quedgeley	By KATHLEEN MORGAN	215
Randwick	By N. M. HERBERT	224
Standish	By C. R. ELRINGTON	230
King's Stanley	By N. M. HERBERT	242
Leonard Stanley	By N. M. HERBERT	257
Stonehouse	By N. M. HERBERT	267
Wheatenhurst or Whitminster	By C. R. ELRINGTON	289
Index	By N. M. HERBERT	300
Corrigenda to Volumes II, VI, and VIII		323

VOLUME ELEVEN

Edited by N. M. Herbert

(1976)

PAGE

Dedication	v
Contents	ix
List of Illustrations	x
List of Maps and Plans	xii
Editorial Note	xiii
Classes of Documents in the Public Record Office used	xv
Gloucestershire Record Office Accumulations	xvi
Note on Abbreviations	xvii

Topography	Architectural descriptions compiled or revised by A. P. BAGGS	
Bisley Hundred	By N. M. HERBERT	1
Bisley	By N. M. HERBERT	4
Edgeworth	By W. J. SHEILS	41
Miserden	By W. J. SHEILS	47
Painswick	By W. J. SHEILS	56
Sapperton	By W. J. SHEILS	87
Stroud	By N. M. HERBERT	99
Winstone	By W. J. SHEILS	145
Longtree Hundred	By N. M. HERBERT	152
Avening	By W. J. SHEILS	156
Cherington	By A. R. J. JURICA	166
Horsley	By W. J. SHEILS	175
Minchinhampton	By N. M. HERBERT	184
Nailsworth	By N. M. HERBERT and W. J. SHEILS	207
Rodborough	By N. M. HERBERT	218
Rodmarton	By A. R. J. JURICA	234

		PAGE
Shipton Moyne	By A. R. J. Jurica	247
Tetbury	By N. M. Herbert	257
Westonbirt with Lasborough	By A. R. J. Jurica	283
Woodchester	By W. J. Sheils	294
Index		305
Corrigenda to Volumes VI, VIII, and X		339

MIDDLESEX

VOLUME FOUR

Edited by J. S. Cockburn and T. F. T. Baker
(1971)

		PAGE
Dedication		v
Contents		ix
List of Illustrations		x
List of Maps and Plans		xii
Editorial Note		xiii
Middlesex Victoria County History Council		xv
Classes of Documents in the Public Record Office used		xvii
Classes of Documents in the Greater London Record Office (Middlesex Records) used		xviii
Note on Abbreviations		xix
Topography		
Elthorne Hundred *(continued)*		
Harmondsworth	By Gillian Wyld	1
Hayes	By Gillian Wyld	22
Norwood, including Southall	By Gillian Wyld	40
Hillingdon, including Uxbridge	By J. S. Cockburn	55
Ickenham	By H. P. F. King	100
Northolt	By J. S. Cockburn	109
Perivale	By J. S. Cockburn	122
Ruislip	By J. S. Cockburn	127
Gore Hundred *(part)*	By J. S. Cockburn	149
Edgware	By D. C. Yaxley	151
Harrow, including Pinner	By Diane K. Bolton	169
Index	By T. F. T. Baker	271
Corrigenda to Volumes I and III		289

VOLUME FIVE

Edited by T. F. T. Baker
(1976)

	PAGE
Dedication	v
Contents	ix
List of Illustrations	x
List of Maps	xii
Editorial Note	xiii
Middlesex Victoria County History Council	xiv
Classes of Documents in the Public Record Office used	xv
Classes of Documents in the Greater London Record Office (Middlesex Records) used	xvii
Note on Abbreviations	xviii

PAGE

Topography . . . . . Architectural investigation by A. P. BAGGS
  Gore Hundred *(continued)*
    Hendon . . . . . By G. C. TYACK 1
    Kingsbury . . . . . By DIANE K. BOLTON . . . 49
    Great Stanmore . . . . By T. F. T. BAKER . . . 88
    Little Stanmore . . . . By T. F. T. BAKER . . . 110
  Edmonton Hundred 128
    Edmonton . . . . . By DIANE K. BOLTON . . . 130
    Enfield . . . . . By G. C. TYACK . . . 207
    Monken Hadley . . . . By G. C. TYACK . . . 260
    South Mimms . . . . By EILEEN P. SCARFF . . . 271
    Tottenham . . . . . By T. F. T. BAKER . . . 307
Index . . . . . . By DIANE K. BOLTON . . . 381
Corrigenda to Volumes I, II, and IV 423

VOLUME SIX

Edited by T. F. T. Baker
(1980)

PAGE

Dedication v
Contents ix
List of Illustrations x
List of Maps xii
Editorial Note xiii
Middlesex Victoria County History Council xiv
Classes of Documents in the Public Record Office used xv
Classes of Documents in the Greater London Record Office (Middlesex Records) used . . xvi
Note on Abbreviations xvii
Topography . . . . . Architectural investigation by A. P. BAGGS
  Ossulstone Hundred . . . . By R. B. PUGH, D.LIT. . . . 1
    Friern Barnet . . . . By M. A. HICKS . . . 6
    Finchley . . . . . By DIANE K. BOLTON . . . 38
    Hornsey, including Highgate . . By T. F. T. BAKER and M. A. HICKS . 101
Index . . . . . . By T. F. T. BAKER . . 206
Corrigenda to Volumes III and V 227

VOLUME SEVEN

Acton, Chiswick, Ealing, and Willesden Parishes
Edited by T. F. T. Baker
(1982)

PAGE

Dedication v
Contents ix
List of Illustrations x
List of Maps xii
Editorial Note xiii
Middlesex Victoria County History Council xiv
Classes of Documents in the Public Record Office used xv
Classes of Documents in the Greater London Record Office used xvii
Note on Abbreviations xviii
Topography . . . . . Architectural investigation by A. P. BAGGS
  Ossulstone Hundred *(continued)*
    Acton . . . . . By PATRICIA E. C. CROOT . . 1

PAGE

Chiswick	By T. F. T. Baker	50
Ealing and Brentford	By M. A. Hicks	100
West Twyford	By Diane K. Bolton	172
Willesden	By Diane K. Bolton	177
Index	By Patricia E. C. Croot	255
Corrigenda to Volumes IV, V, and VI		280

VOLUME EIGHT
Islington and Stoke Newington Parishes
Edited by T. F. T. Baker
(1985)

PAGE

Dedication		v
Contents		ix
List of Illustrations		x
List of Maps		xii
Editorial Note		xiii
Middlesex Victoria County History Committee		xiv
Classes of Documents in the Public Record Office used		xv
Classes of Documents in the Greater London Record Office used		xvii
Note on Abbreviations		xviii
Topography	Architectural investigation by A. P. Baggs	
Ossulstone Hundred *(continued)*		
Islington	By Patricia E. C. Croot	1
Stoke Newington	By Diane K. Bolton	139
Index	By Patricia E. C. Croot	227
Corrigenda to Volumes V, VI, and VII		245

VOLUME NINE
Hampstead and Paddington Parishes
Edited by T. F. T. Baker
(1989)

PAGE

Dedication		v
Contents		ix
List of Illustrations		xi
List of Maps		xiii
Middlesex Victoria County History Committee		xiv
Editorial Note		xv
Classes of Documents in the Public Record Office used		xvi
Classes of Documents in the Greater London Record Office used		xvii
Note on Abbreviations		xviii
Topography	Architectural investigation by A. P. Baggs	
Ossulstone Hundred *(continued)*		
Hampstead	By Diane K. Bolton; Public Services, Churches, Roman Catholicism, Protestant Nonconformity, Judaism, Education, and Charities by Patricia E. C. Croot; Hampstead Heath, Social Activities, Trade and Industry, and part of Communications by T. F. T. Baker	1
Communications		3

CONTENTS OF VOLUMES: MIDDX. IX

PAGE

Settlement and Growth 8
  Hampstead Town 15
  Frognal and the Central Demesne 33
  West End 42
  Kilburn, Edgware Road, and Cricklewood 47
  Belsize 51
  St. John's Wood 60
  Chalcots 63
  North End, Littleworth, and Spaniard's End 66
  Vale of Health 71
  Childs Hill 73
  Hampstead Heath 75
Social and Cultural Activities 81
Manor and Other Estates 92
Economic History
  Agriculture 111
  Woods 121
  Mills 122
  Fairs 123
  Trade and Industry 123
Local Government
  Manorial Government 130
  Parish Government to 1837 132
  Local Government after 1837 135
Public Services 138
Churches 145
Roman Catholicism 152
Protestant Nonconformity 153
Judaism 158
Buddhism 159
Sikhism 159
Other Faiths 159
Education 159
Charities for the Poor 169
Paddington . . . . . By T. F. T. Baker . . . 173
Communications 174
Growth
  Settlement and Building to c. 1800 181
  Building after c. 1800 182
  Paddington Green 185
  Tyburnia 190
  Westbourne Green 198
  Bayswater 204
  Maida Vale 212
  Queen's Park and St. Peter's Park 217
Social and Cultural Activities 221
Manors and Other Estates 226
Economic History
  Agriculture 233
  Nurseries and Market Gardens 235
  Woods 235
  Trade and Industry 236
Local Government
  Manorial Government 241
  Parish Government to 1837 241
  Local Government after 1837 243

		PAGE
Public Services .	. . . .	246
Churches	. . . .	252
Roman Catholicism	. . . .	259
Protestant Nonconformity	. . . .	260
Greek Orthodox Church	. . . .	264
Judaism	. . . .	264
Education	. . . .	265
Charities for the Poor	. . . .	271
Index	. . . .	273
Corrigenda to Volumes I, III–VI, and VIII .	. . . .	302

OXFORDSHIRE

VOLUME FOUR
The City of Oxford
Edited by Alan Crossley
(1979)

		PAGE
Dedication .	. . . .	v
Contents	. . . .	ix
List of Illustrations .	. . . .	xi
List of Maps and Plans	. . . .	xii
Editorial Note	. . . .	xiii
Classes of Documents in the Public Record Office used	. . . . . .	xiv
Principal Bodleian Manuscripts used	. . . . . .	xv
Note on the Oxford City Archives .	. . . .	xvii
Note on Abbreviations	. . . .	xviii
The City of Oxford		Architectural descriptions written in collaboration with A. P. Baggs	
Introduction	. . . . .	By A. Crossley	1
Medieval Oxford .	. . . .	By Janet Cooper; Economic History by Janet Cooper and A. Crossley .	3
Early Modern Oxford	. . . .	By A. Crossley; Religious Life by Janet Cooper, Parliamentary Representation after 1660 by Christina Colvin .	74
Modern Oxford .	. . . .	By C. J. Day; Religious Life by Janet Cooper, Parliamentary Representation by Christina Colvin . .	181
Boundaries	. . . .	By Janet Cooper . . .	260
Outlying Parts of the Liberty	. . .	By Janet Cooper; Port Meadow by A. Crossley . . .	265
Communications .	. . .	By C. J. Day . . .	284
Castle	. . . .	By Janet Cooper . . .	296
City Walls, Gates, and Posterns .	. .	By T. G. Hassall . . .	300
The King's Houses	. . .	By A. Crossley . . .	304
Markets and Fairs	. . .	By Janet Cooper . . .	305
Craft Guilds .	. . .	By A. Crossley . . .	312
Mills and Fisheries	. . .	By Janet Cooper . . .	327
Municipal Buildings	. . .	By Janet Cooper . . .	331
Courts .	. . .	By Janet Cooper and A. Crossley .	336
City Arms, Plate, Seals, and Insignia	.	By Janet Cooper . . .	340
Parish Government and Poor-Relief	.	By A. Crossley and Christina Colvin .	342

PAGE

Public Services . . . . . By Nesta Selwyn, A. Crossley, C. J. Day, and Mary Jessup . . . 350
Sites and Remains of Religious Houses . . By Janet Cooper . . . 364
Churches . . . . . . By Janet Cooper . . . 369
Roman Catholicism . . . . By Christina Colvin . . 412
Protestant Nonconformity and Other Christian Bodies By Christina Colvin . . 415
Non-Christian Religious Bodies . . . By Christina Colvin . . 425
Social and Cultural Activities . . . By Nesta Selwyn . . . 425
Education . . . . . By Nesta Selwyn . . . 442
Charities for the Poor . . . . By A. Crossley . . . 462
Street-Names . . . . . By Janet Cooper . . . 475
Index . . . . . . By Eleanor Chance, A. Crossley, Janet Cooper, and C. J. Day . . 478

VOLUME TEN
Banbury Hundred
Edited by Alan Crossley
(1972)

PAGE

Dedication v
Contents ix
List of Illustrations xi
List of Maps and Plans xiii
Editorial Note xv
Classes of Documents in the Public Record Office used xvii
Principal Bodleian Manuscripts used xix
Note on Abbreviations xxi
Topography . . . . . Where not otherwise stated, by the Oxfordshire Editorial Staff, namely A. Crossley, Judith Hook, Hilary Turner, Mary Jessup, and Janet Cooper
Banbury Hundred . . . . By Janet Cooper . . . 1
Banbury . . . . . Introduction, Growth of the Town, Manors, Economic History, and Local Government to 1554, by P. D. A. Harvey; Parliamentary Representation by Christina Colvin (1554–1830) and B. S. Trinder (1830–85); Protestant Nonconformity by B. S. Trinder; Buildings from 1700 by N. H. Cooper . 5
Charlbury . . . . . By the late Marjory Hollings and the Oxfordshire Editorial Staff . 127
Cropredy . . . . . By J. F. A. Mason . . 157
Cropredy . . . . . By J. F. A. Mason . . 160
Great and Little Bourton . . . By J. F. A. Mason . . 175
Claydon . . . . . By J. F. A. Mason . . 184
Clattercote . . . . . By J. F. A. Mason . . 194
Mollington . . . . . By J. F. A. Mason . . 197
Prescote . . . . . By J. F. A. Mason . . 206
Wardington . . . . . By J. F. A. Mason . . 210
Swalcliffe . . . . . By Mary D. Lobel and the Oxfordshire Editorial Staff . . . 225
Index 261

VOLUME ELEVEN
Wootton Hundred (Northern Part)
Edited by Alan Crossley
(1983)

	PAGE
Dedication	v
Contents	ix
List of Illustrations	x
List of Maps and Plans	xii
Editorial Note	xiii
Classes of Documents in the Public Record Office used	xv
Principal Bodleian Manuscripts used	xvii
Note on Abbreviations	xix

Topography . . . . . Nonconformity and Poor Relief prepared by CHRISTINA COLVIN, Education and Charities by NESTA SELWYN. Architectural descriptions written or revised by A. P. BAGGS

		PAGE
Wootton Hundred	By A. CROSSLEY	1
North Aston	By C. J. DAY	6
Steeple Aston	By C. J. DAY	21
Barford St. Michael	By A. TOMKINSON and A. CROSSLEY	45
Steeple Barton	By JANET COOPER	59
Westcott Barton	By JANET COOPER	75
Deddington	By H. M. COLVIN and A. CROSSLEY	81
Glympton	By JANET COOPER	120
Heythrop	By C. J. DAY	131
South Newington	By JANET COOPER	143
Rousham	By JANET COOPER	159
Sandford St. Martin	By JANET COOPER	169
Stonesfield	By C. J. DAY	181
Tackley	By JANET COOPER	194
Duns Tew	By A. TOMKINSON and C. J. DAY	209
Great Tew	By A. TOMKINSON and A. CROSSLEY	223
Little Tew	By A. TOMKINSON and C. J. DAY	247
Wootton	By A. CROSSLEY	259
Nether Worton	By A. TOMKINSON and A. CROSSLEY	285
Over Worton	By A. TOMKINSON and A. CROSSLEY	293
Index		301

VOLUME TWELVE
Wootton Hundred (South) including Woodstock
Edited by Alan Crossley
(1990)

	PAGE
Dedication	iv
Contents	vii
List of Illustrations	viii
List of Maps and Plans	x
Editorial Note	xiii
Oxfordshire Victoria History: key map to volumes published	xiv
Classes of Documents in the Public Record Office used	xv
Select List of Bodleian Library Manuscripts used	xvii
Note on Abbreviations	xix

PAGE

Topography . . . . . Nonconformity and Poor Relief prepared
by CHRISTINA COLVIN, Education and
Charities by NESTA SELWYN.
Architectural descriptions written or
revised by A. P. BAGGS

Wootton Hundred (southern part) . . . By A. CROSSLEY 1
  Begbroke . . . . . By C. J. DAY 3
  Bladon . . . . . By JANET COOPER 14
  Cassington . . . . . By JANET COOPER 36
  Cogges . . . . . By W. J. BLAIR and S. C. TOWNLEY . 54
  Combe . . . . . By C. J. DAY 75
  Eynsham . . . . . By A. CROSSLEY 98
  Hanborough . . . . . By JANET COOPER 158
  Kidlington . . . . . By JANET COOPER 179
  North Leigh . . . . . By C. J. DAY 213
  South Leigh . . . . . By S. C. TOWNLEY 238
  Shipton-on-Cherwell . . . . By JANET COOPER 254
  Stanton Harcourt . . . . By S. C. TOWNLEY 267
  Wilcote . . . . . By C. J. DAY 296
  Wolvercote . . . . . By T. G. HASSALL and JANET COOPER . 304
  Woodstock . . . . . By A. CROSSLEY 325
    Woodstock . . . . . A. CROSSLEY, with S. C. TOWNLEY (Local
Government: Reformed Borough) and
CHRISTINA COLVIN (Parliamentary
Representation from 1660) . . 326
  Old Woodstock . . . . By C. J. DAY 423
  Blenheim . . . . . By A. CROSSLEY 430
  Yarnton . . . . . By C. J. DAY 470
Index . . . . . . By ELEANOR CHANCE, A. CROSSLEY, C. J.
DAY, and S. C. TOWNLEY . . 491

SHROPSHIRE

VOLUME TWO

Edited by A. T. Gaydon
(1973)

PAGE

Dedication v
Contents ix
List of Illustrations xiii
List of Maps xv
Editorial Note xvii
Classes of Documents in the Public Record Office used xviii
Accumulations and Collections in the Shropshire Record Office used xix
Note on Abbreviations xx
Ecclesiastical Organization . . . . By the Revd. D. T. W. PRICE . 1
Religious Houses . . . . . Architectural descriptions compiled or
revised by MARGARET TOMLINSON
  Introduction . . . . . By MARJORIE M. CHIBNALL and A. T.
GAYDON 18
  Houses of Benedictine Monks . . . By MARJORIE M. CHIBNALL
    1. The Priory of Bromfield 27
    2. The Priory of Morville 29
    3. The Abbey of Shrewsbury 30

CONTENTS OF VOLUMES: SALOP. II

PAGE

Houses of Cluniac Monks . . . By Marjorie M. Chibnall
   4. The Priory of Preen 38
   5. The Abbey, later Priory, of Wenlock 38
House of Grandmontine Monks . . . By Marjorie M. Chibnall
   6. The Priory of Alberbury 47
House of Cistercian Monks . . . By Marjorie M. Chibnall
   7. The Abbey of Buildwas 50
Houses of Augustinian Canons . . . By Marjorie M. Chibnall
   8. The Priory of Chirbury 59
   9. The Abbey of Haughmond 62
   10. The Abbey of Lilleshall 70
   11. The Priory of Ratlinghope 80
   12. The Priory of Wombridge 80
House of Augustinian Canonesses . . . By Marjorie M. Chibnall
   13. The Priory of St. Leonard, Brewood 83
House of Knights Templars . . . By A. T. Gaydon
   14. The Preceptory of Lydley 85
House of Knights Hospitallers . . . By A. T. Gaydon
   15. The Preceptory of Halston 87
Friaries . . . . . By Marjorie M. Chibnall
   16. The Franciscan Friars of Bridgnorth 89
   17. The Franciscan Friars of Shrewsbury 89
   18. The Dominican Friars of Shrewsbury 91
   19. The Carmelite Friars of Ludlow 93
   20. The Austin Friars of Ludlow 95
   21. The Austin Friars of Shrewsbury 96
   22. The Austin Friars of Woodhouse 97
Hospitals . . . . . By A. T. Gaydon
   23. Bridgnorth, Holy Trinity and St. John 98
   24. Bridgnorth, St. James 100
   25. Ludford, St. Giles 101
   26. Ludlow, St. John 102
   27. Oswestry, St. John 104
   28. Shrewsbury, St. George 105
   29. Shrewsbury, St. Giles 106
   30. Shrewsbury, St. John 106
Almshouses . . . . . By A. T. Gaydon
   31. Ludlow, Hosier's Almshouses 108
   32. Newport, the Town Almshouses 110
   33. Shrewsbury, the Mercers' (or St. Chad's) Almshouses 110
   34. Shrewsbury, the Drapers' (or St. Mary's) Almshouses 111
Colleges . . . . . By A. T. Gaydon
   35. Shrewsbury, St. Chad 114
   36. Shrewsbury, St. Mary 119
   37. Bridgnorth, St. Mary Magdalen 123
   38. Battlefield, St. Mary Magdalen 128
   39. Tong, St. Bartholomew 131
   40. Newport, St. Mary 133
Religious Guild . . . . . By A. T. Gaydon
   41. Ludlow, Palmers' Guild 134
Public Schools and Endowed Grammar Schools . By the Revd. D. T. W. Price; Ludlow Grammar School by A. T. Gaydon and D. T. W. Price; architectural descriptions compiled or revised by Margaret Tomlinson
   1. Bitterley Grammar School 141
   2. Bridgnorth Grammar School 142

PAGE

3. Donnington, formerly Wroxeter, Grammar School 143
4. Market Drayton Grammar School 145
5. High Ercall Grammar School 146
6. Ludlow Grammar School 147
7. Adams' Grammar School, Newport 150
8. Oswestry School 152
9. Shifnal Grammar School 153
10. Shrewsbury School 154
11. Adams' Grammar School, Wem 158
12. Sir John Talbot's Grammar School, Whitchurch 159
13. Worfield Grammar School 161
14. Ellesmere College 162
15. Wrekin College 163
16. The Careswell Foundation 164
Sport
Introduction . . . . . By A. T. GAYDON 165
Fox-Hunting . . . . . By M. J. ANGOLD 166
Horse-Racing . . . . . By M. J. ANGOLD and A. T. GAYDON . 177
Coursing . . . . . . By the Revd. D. T. W. PRICE . . 183
Otter-Hunting . . . . . By the Revd. D. T. W. PRICE . . 185
Fishing . . . . . . By the Revd. D. T. W. PRICE . . 186
Shooting . . . . . . By A. T. GAYDON and the Revd. D. T. W.
PRICE 188
Cock-Fighting and Bull-Baiting . . . By B. S. TRINDER 190
Athletics . . . . . . By A. T. GAYDON 192
Cricket . . . . . . By M. J. ANGOLD and A. T. GAYDON . 194
Association Football . . . . By A. T. GAYDON 197
Rowing . . . . . . By A. T. GAYDON 201
Population Table . . . . . By M. J. ANGOLD and A. T. GAYDON . 204
Index to the text of Shropshire Domesday . By the Revd. D. T. W. PRICE . . 238
Index to Volumes I and II . . . By G. C. BAUGH, the Revd. D. T. W.
PRICE, and D. C. COX . . 246
Corrigenda to Volume I 315

VOLUME THREE
Edited by G. C. Baugh
(1979)

PAGE

Dedication v
Contents ix
List of Illustrations xi
List of Maps xii
Editorial Note xiii
Classes of Documents in the Public Record Office used xiv
Accumulations and Collections in the Shropshire Record Office used . . xv
Note on Abbreviations xvi
County Government in the Early Middle Ages . By D. C. COX . . . 1
The Franchises . . . . . By G. C. BAUGH . . . 33
County Government 1327–1603 . . . By D. C. COX . . . 54
County Government 1603–1714 . . . By D. C. COX . . . 90
County Government 1714–1834 . . . By G. C. BAUGH . . . 115
County Government 1834–89 . . . By G. C. BAUGH . . . 135
The New Local Authorities . . . By G. C. BAUGH . . . 167
The County Council 1889–1974 . . . By D. C. COX . . . 181
Law and Order after 1889 . . . By D. C. COX . . . 224

PAGE

Parliamentary Representation . . . By J. F. A. Mason (Shropshire to 1629 by
D. C. Cox) 232

    To 1629 232

    1640–60 249

    1660–1832 254

    1832–85 308

    1885–1918 343

    1918–74 354

Officers, Seals, and Arms . . . . By G. C. Baugh 359

Index . . . . By G. C. Baugh and D. C. Cox . 363

Corrigenda to Volumes I and II 398

VOLUME FOUR
Agriculture
Edited by G. C. Baugh
(1989)

PAGE

Dedication v

Contents ix

List of Illustrations xi

List of Maps and other Figures xiii

List of Tables xiv

Editorial Note xv

Classes of Documents in the Public Record Office used xvi

Accumulations and Collections in the Shropshire Record Office used xvii

Note on Abbreviations xviii

Agriculture 1

   The Physical Environment . . . By Trevor Rowley . . . 5

   Early Agriculture . . . . By P. A. Stamper . . . 20

   Domesday Book to 1300 . . . By P. A. Stamper . . . 26

     Lords and tenants 27

     Woodland, assarting, and commons 40

     Arable farming 48

     Livestock and pastoral farming 53

     Marketing 65

   1300–1540 . . . . By Ann J. Kettle . . . 72

     Landlords 77

     Assarting and inclosure 80

     Demesne agriculture 85

     The leasing of the demesnes 103

     Peasants 107

   1540–1750 . . . . By P. R. Edwards . . . 119

     Inclosure 119

     Landlord and tenant 128

     Arable farming 141

     Livestock and dairy farming 150

     Marketing 161

   1750–1875 . . . . By G. C. Baugh and R. C. Hill . 168

     Inclosure 171

     The Agricultural Revolution 177

     Motive power, tools, and mechanization 188

     Livestock breeds 196

     The large estates 202

     Landlords and tenants 212

     Labourers and cottagers 220

PAGE

1875–1985 . . . . . By R. Perren 232
  Arable farming 237
  Dairy farming 241
  Livestock rearing and feeding 246
  Agrarian economy and society 250
  Agricultural education 265
Index . . . . . . By G. C. Baugh, D. C. Cox, and P. A.
                        Stamper . . . 270
Corrigenda to Volumes I–III 293

VOLUME ELEVEN
Telford
Edited by G. C. Baugh
(1985)

PAGE

Dedication v
Contents ix
List of Illustrations x
List of Maps and Plans xii
Editorial Note xiii
Classes of Documents in the Public Record Office used xv
Accumulations and Collections in the Shropshire Record Office used . . . xvii
Note on Abbreviations xix
Topography . . . . . Architectural descriptions prepared in
                        collaboration with A. P. Baggs

  Telford . . . . . By G. C. Baugh 1
  The Liberty and Borough of Wenlock *(part)*
    Madeley including Coalbrookdale, Coalport,
      and Ironbridge . . . By G. C. Baugh . . . 21
    Little Wenlock . . . . By D. C. Cox . . . 77
  Bradford Hundred . . . By G. C. Baugh . . . 93
    Parishes forming part of the Southern Division
    Dawley . . . . By A. J. L. Winchester . . 105
    Eyton upon the Weald Moors . . By A. J. L. Winchester . . 136
    Lilleshall . . . . By D. C. Cox . . . 145
    Preston upon the Weald Moors . . By P. A. Stamper; Education by Jessie
                      McFall . . . 176
    Stirchley . . . . By A. J. L. Winchester . . 184
    Wellington . . . . By D. C. Cox; Education by Jessie
                      McFall . . . 197
      Hadley and Horton 253
      Ketley 267
      Lawley 276
    Wombridge, later Oakengates . . By P. A. Stamper; Education by Jessie
                      McFall . . . 286
    Wrockwardine . . . . By P. A. Stamper; Education by Jessie
                      McFall . . . 306
      Wrockwardine Wood 323
Index . . . . . By G. C. Baugh, D. C. Cox, and P. A.
                      Stamper . . . 337
Corrigenda to Volumes I–III, VIII 375

SOMERSET

VOLUME THREE
Edited by R. W. Dunning
(1974)

		PAGE
Dedication	.	v
Contents	.	ix
List of Illustrations	.	xi
List of Maps and Plans	.	xiii
Editorial Note	.	xv
Classes of Documents in the Public Record Office used	.	xvii
Somerset Record Office Accumulations	.	xviii
Note on Abbreviations	.	xix
Somerset Record Society Publications	.	xxi
Topography	Architectural descriptions prepared in collaboration with MARGARET TOMLINSON and A. P. BAGGS	
Kingsbury (East) Hundred	By R. W. DUNNING	1
Huish Episcopi	By R. W. DUNNING	1
Pitney Hundred	By R. W. DUNNING	14
Langport	By R. J. E. BUSH	16
Muchelney	By R. W. DUNNING	38
Pitney	By R. W. DUNNING	50
Somerton Hundred	By R. J. E. BUSH	57
Aller	By R. J. E. BUSH	61
West Camel	By R. W. DUNNING	71
Charlton Adam	By R. J. E. BUSH	81
Charlton Mackrell	By R. J. E. BUSH	95
Kingsdon	By R. J. E. BUSH	111
East Lydford	By R. J. E. BUSH	120
Somerton	By R. W. DUNNING	129
Long Sutton	By R. W. DUNNING	154
Yeovilton	By R. W. DUNNING	166
Tintinhull Hundred	By R. W. DUNNING	176
Ilchester	By R. W. DUNNING	179
Kingstone	By R. W. DUNNING	203
Montacute	By R. W. DUNNING	210
Northover	By R. W. DUNNING	224
Sock Dennis	By R. W. DUNNING	230
Stoke sub Hamdon	By R. W. DUNNING	235
Thorne	By R. W. DUNNING	250
Tintinhull	By R. W. DUNNING	255
Index	.	266

VOLUME FOUR
Edited by R. W. Dunning
(1978)

		PAGE
Dedication	.	v
Contents	.	ix
List of Illustrations	.	xi
List of Maps and Plans	.	xiii
Editorial Note	.	xv

			PAGE
Classes of Documents in the Public Record Office used	.	.	xvii
Somerset Record Office Accumulations	.	.	xviii
Note on Abbreviations	.	.	xix
Somerset Record Society Publications	.	.	xx
Topography	Architectural descriptions prepared in collaboration with A. P. BAGGS		
Crewkerne Hundred	By R. W. DUNNING	.	1
Crewkerne	By R. W. DUNNING and R. J. E. BUSH	.	4
Hinton St. George	By R. W. DUNNING	.	38
Merriott	By R. J. E. BUSH	.	52
Misterton	By R. J. E. BUSH	.	62
Wayford	By R. J. E. BUSH	.	68
Martock Hundred	By R. J. E. BUSH	.	76
Martock	By R. J. E. BUSH	.	78
South Petherton Hundred	By R. W. DUNNING	.	111
Barrington	By R. W. DUNNING	.	113
Chaffcombe	By R. J. E. BUSH	.	121
Chillington	By R. W. DUNNING	.	128
Cricket St. Thomas	By R. J. E. BUSH	.	133
Cudworth	By R. W. DUNNING	.	141
Dinnington	By R. W. DUNNING	.	147
Dowlish Wake	By R. J. E. BUSH	.	151
Knowle St. Giles	By R. J. E. BUSH	.	156
Lopen	By R. W. DUNNING	.	163
South Petherton	By R. W. DUNNING	.	170
Seavington St. Mary	By R. W. DUNNING	.	198
Seavington St. Michael	By R. W. DUNNING	.	205
Shepton Beauchamp	By R. J. E. BUSH	.	210
Wambrook	By R. J. E. BUSH	.	222
Whitestaunton	By R. J. E. BUSH	.	231
Index	By R. W. DUNNING	.	239

VOLUME FIVE

Edited by R. W. Dunning

(1985)

			PAGE
Dedication	.	.	v
Contents	.	.	ix
List of Illustrations	.	.	xi
List of Maps and Plans	.	.	xii
Editorial Note	.	.	xiii
Classes of Documents in the Public Record Office used	.	.	xiv
Somerset Record Office Accumulations	.	.	xv
Note on Abbreviations	.	.	xvii
Somerset Record Society Publications	.	.	xix
Topography	Architectural descriptions prepared in collaboration with A. P. BAGGS		
Whitley Hundred (part)	By R. W. DUNNING	.	1
Holford	By R. W. DUNNING	.	2
Williton and Freemanors Hundred (eastern part)	By R. W. DUNNING	.	7
Bicknoller	By MARY S. SIRAUT	.	13
Brompton Ralph	By MARY S. SIRAUT	.	19
Chipstable	By R. W. DUNNING	.	26
Clatworthy	By R. J. E. BUSH	.	31
Old Cleeve	By R. W. DUNNING	.	39
Crowcombe	By R. J. E. BUSH	.	54

PAGE

Dodington	By R. W. Dunning		65
Elworthy	By Mary S. Siraut		69
Halse	By R. W. Dunning		73
Huish Champflower	By R. W. Dunning		81
Kilton	By R. W. Dunning		88
Kilve	By R. W. Dunning		96
Lilstock	By R. W. Dunning		103
Monksilver	By Mary S. Siraut		107
Nettlecombe	By Mary S. Siraut		111
East Quantoxhead	By R. W. Dunning		120
West Quantoxhead	By R. W. Dunning		129
Raddington	By R. W. Dunning		136
St. Decumans, including Watchet and Williton	By R. W. Dunning		143
Sampford Brett	By Mary S. Siraut		171
Stogumber	By Mary S. Siraut		177
Nether Stowey	By Mary S. Siraut		190
Index	By R. W. Dunning		201

STAFFORDSHIRE

VOLUME SIX

Edited by M. W. Greenslade and D. A. Johnson
(1979)

PAGE

Dedication		v
Contents		ix
List of Illustrations		x
List of Maps and Plans		xii
Editorial Note		xiii
Staffordshire Victoria County History Committee		xiv
Classes of Documents in the Public Record Office		xv
Note on Abbreviations		xvi
Analysis of Sources in *Collections for a History of Staffordshire*		xviii
Medieval Agriculture	By Jean R. Birrell	1
Agriculture 1500 to 1793	By Ann J. Kettle	49
Agriculture 1793 to 1875	By C. R. J. Currie	91
Agriculture 1875 to 1975	By C. R. J. Currie	122
Schools		
Brewood Grammar School	By D. A. Johnson	149
The School of St. Mary and St. Anne, Abbots Bromley	By C. R. J. Currie	152
Burton-upon-Trent Grammar School	By C. R. J. Currie	154
Cotton College, formerly Sedgley Park School	By M. W. Greenslade	156
Denstone College	By D. A. Johnson and C. R. J. Currie	158
Lichfield Grammar School	By C. R. J. Currie	159
Newcastle-under-Lyme Grammar School	By M. W. Greenslade	161
Rugeley Grammar School	By C. R. J. Currie	162
King Edward VI Grammar School, Stafford	By D. A. Johnson	164
Alleyne's Grammar School, Stone	By D. A. Johnson	167
Queen Elizabeth's Grammar School, Tamworth	By D. A. Johnson	168
Tettenhall College	By C. R. J. Currie	171
Alleyne's Grammar School, Uttoxeter	By D. A. Johnson	172

PAGE

Queen Mary's Grammar School, Walsall . . By D. A. JOHNSON and C. R. J. CURRIE . 174
Wolverhampton Grammar School . . By D. A. JOHNSON and C. R. J. CURRIE . 177
The Royal Wolverhampton School . . By C. R. J. CURRIE . . . 179
The University of Keele . . . . By C. R. J. CURRIE . . . 182
The Borough of Stafford . . . . By M. W. GREENSLADE with D. A. JOHNSON
and C. R. J. CURRIE. Castle, gaols, and
houses of correction by R. B. PUGH,
D.LIT. Architectural descriptions
prepared in collaboration with A. P.
BAGGS . 185
Index 275

VOLUME FOURTEEN
Lichfield
Edited by M. W. Greenslade
(1990)

PAGE

Dedication iv
Contents vii
List of Plates ix
List of Figures xi
Staffordshire Victoria History: key map to volumes published xii
Editorial Note xiii
Staffordshire Victoria History Committee xiv
Classes of Documents in the Public Record Office xv
Main Classes of Documents in the Lichfield Joint Record Office xvi
Note on Abbreviations xvii
Analysis of Sources in Collections for a History of Staffordshire xxi
Topography . . . . . Architectural descriptions prepared in
collaboration with A. P. BAGGS

The City of Lichfield
Introduction . . . . . By M. W. GREENSLADE . . . 1
General History . . . . By M. W. GREENSLADE . . . 4
Early Settlement 4
The Anglo-Saxon Ecclesiastical Centre . (with D. A. JOHNSON) . . 5
The 12th Century 9
The 13th Century 10
The Late Middle Ages 11
From the Reformation to the Civil War 14
The Civil War 17
From the Restoration to the End of
the 18th Century . . . (by N. J. TRINGHAM) . . 18
The 19th Century 24
The 20th Century 32
The Place Name . . . . By D. A. JOHNSON . . . 37
Population . . . . . By M. W. GREENSLADE . . . 39
Boundaries and Gates . . . By N. J. TRINGHAM . . . 39
Street Names . . . . By N. J. TRINGHAM . . . 40
Domestic Buildings . . . By A. P. BAGGS . . . 43
Communications . . . By M. W. GREENSLADE . . . 44
The Cathedral and the Close . . By N. J. TRINGHAM . . . 47
Manor and Other Estates . . By N. J. TRINGHAM; Beacon Place, Stowe
House, and Stowe Hill by M. W.
GREENSLADE . . . 67
Town Government . . . By N. J. TRINGHAM . . . 73
Parish Government and Poor Relief . . By M. W. GREENSLADE . . . 87

PAGE

Parliamentary Representation	By N. J. TRINGHAM	92
Public Services .	By M. W. GREENSLADE	95
Economic History	By N. J. TRINGHAM; Mills and Markets and Fairs by M. W. GREENSLADE	109
Guilds .	By M. W. GREENSLADE and N. J. TRINGHAM	131
Churches	By D. A. JOHNSON; individual parish churches by M. W. GREENSLADE	134
Roman Catholicism	By M. W. GREENSLADE	155
Protestant Nonconformity	By N. J. TRINGHAM	156
Social and Cultural Activities	By N. J. TRINGHAM	159
Education	By D. A. JOHNSON .	170
Charities for the Poor	By D. A. JOHNSON .	184
Outlying Townships of Lichfield .	Education and Charities for the Poor by D. A. JOHNSON .	195
Burntwood	By M. W. GREENSLADE	195
Curborough and Elmhurst	By N. J. TRINGHAM	229
Fisherwick with Tamhorn	By M. W. GREENSLADE	237
Freeford	By N. J. TRINGHAM	253
Hammerwich	By M. W. GREENSLADE	258
Streethay	By N. J. TRINGHAM	273
Wall with Pipehill	By N. J. TRINGHAM	283
Index		295

VOLUME SEVENTEEN

Edited by M. W. Greenslade

(1976)

PAGE

Dedication .	v
Contents	ix
List of Illustrations .	x
List of Maps and Plans	xiii
Editorial Note	xv
Staffordshire Victoria County History Committee	xvii
Classes of Documents in the Public Record Office	xix
Classes of Official Documents in the Staffordshire Record Office and of documents in the Lichfield Joint Record Office and the Lichfield Diocesan Registry	xx
Note on Abbreviations	xxi
Analysis of Sources in *Collections for a History of Staffordshire*	xxiii

Topography	Architectural descriptions prepared in collaboration with A. P. BAGGS	
Offlow Hundred *(part)*		
West Bromwich	By G.C. BAUGH, M. W. GREENSLADE, and D. A. JOHNSON	1
Smethwick	By G.C. BAUGH, M. W. GREENSLADE, and D. A. JOHNSON	87
Walsall .	By C. R. J. CURRIE, M. W. GREENSLADE, and D. A. JOHNSON	143
Walsall Wood		275
Index		285

VOLUME TWENTY
Seisdon Hundred (Part)
Edited by M. W. Greenslade
(1984)

	PAGE
Dedication	v
Contents	ix
List of Illustrations	x
List of Maps and Plans	xii
Editorial Note	xiii
Staffordshire Victoria History Committee	xiv
Classes of Documents in the Public Record Office	xv
Note on Abbreviations	xvi
Analysis of Sources in *Collections for a History of Staffordshire*	xviii
Topography	Architectural descriptions prepared in collaboration with A. P. BAGGS	
Seisdon Hundred, Northern Division *(part)*		
Tettenhall	By M. W. GREENSLADE, D. A. JOHNSON, and N. J. TRINGHAM	1
Seisdon Hundred, Southern Division		
Amblecote	By M. W. GREENSLADE	49
Bobbington	By N. J. TRINGHAM	64
Codsall	By N. J. TRINGHAM, D. A. JOHNSON, and ANN J. KETTLE	76
Enville	By D. A. JOHNSON and N. J. TRINGHAM	91
Kinver	By M. W. GREENSLADE, D. A. JOHNSON, and N. J. TRINGHAM	118
Patshall	By M. W. GREENSLADE	161
Pattingham	By M. W. GREENSLADE and N. J. TRINGHAM	172
Trysull	By M. W. GREENSLADE and N. J. TRINGHAM	185
Wombourne	By M. W. GREENSLADE, D. A. JOHNSON, and N. J. TRINGHAM	197
Woodford Grange	By N. J. TRINGHAM	225
Index	227

SUSSEX

VOLUME SIX, PART ONE
Bramber Rape (Southern Part)
Edited by T. P. Hudson
(1980)

	PAGE
Dedication	v
Contents	ix
List of Illustrations	x
List of Maps and Plans	xii
Editorial Note	xiii
Classes of Documents in the Public Record Office	xv
Classes of Documents in the Sussex Record Offices	xvi
Collections in the Keeping of the Sussex Archaeological Society	xvi
Note on Abbreviations	xvii

PAGE

Topography . . . . . Architectural descriptions compiled or
                        revised by A. P. BAGGS

Bramber Rape	.	.	.	By T. P. HUDSON	.	.	.	1
Brightford Hundred	.	.	.	By T. P. HUDSON	.	.	.	8
Clapham	.	.	.	By T. P. HUDSON	.	.	.	10
Findon	.	.	.	By T. P. HUDSON	.	.	.	21
Lancing	.	.	.	By T. P. HUDSON	.	.	.	34
Sompting	.	.	.	By SUSAN M. KEELING	.	.	.	53
Worthing and associated parishes	.	.	.	.	.	.	65
Broadwater	.	.	.	By A. M. ROWLAND	.	.	.	66
Durrington	.	.	.	By T. P. HUDSON	.	.	.	81
Heene	.	.	.	By T. P. HUDSON	.	.	.	85
Worthing	.	.	.	By A. M. ROWLAND	.	.	.	92
Fishersgate Half-Hundred	.	.	.	By C. R. ELRINGTON	.	.	.	131
Kingston by Sea	.	.	.	By C. R. ELRINGTON	.	.	.	132
Old and New Shoreham	.	.	.	By C. R. ELRINGTON	.	.	.	138
Southwick	.	.	.	By C. R. ELRINGTON	.	.	.	173
Patching Hundred	.	.	.	By T. P. HUDSON	.	.	.	184
Patching	.	.	.	By T. P. HUDSON	.	.	.	185
Steyning Hundred	.	.	.	By T. P. HUDSON	.	.	.	193
Botolphs	.	.	.	By T. P. HUDSON	.	.	.	195
Bramber	.	.	.	By T. P. HUDSON	.	.	.	201
Coombes	.	.	.	By T. P. HUDSON	.	.	.	215
Steyning	.	.	.	By T. P. HUDSON	.	.	.	220
Washington	.	.	.	By T. P. HUDSON	.	.	.	247
Wiston	.	.	.	By T. P. HUDSON	.	.	.	259
Tarring Hundred	.	.	.	By T. P. HUDSON	.	.	.	269
West Tarring	.	.	.	By T. P. HUDSON	.	.	.	270
Tables	.	.	.	.	.	.	.	281
Index	.	.	.	By T. P. HUDSON	.	.	.	283

VOLUME SIX, PART TWO
Bramber Rape (North-western Part), including Horsham
Edited by T. P. Hudson
(1986)

PAGE

Dedication	.	.	.	.	.	.	.	.	v
Contents	.	.	.	.	.	.	.	.	ix
List of Illustrations	.	.	.	.	.	.	.	.	x
List of Maps	.	.	.	.	.	.	.	.	xii
Editorial Note	.	.	.	.	.	.	.	.	xiii
Classes of Documents in the Public Record Office	.	.	.	.	.	.	xv
Classes of Documents in the Sussex Record Offices	.	.	.	.	.	.	xvi
Sussex Record Society Volumes	.	.	.	.	.	.	.	xvii
Note on Abbreviations	.	.	.	.	.	.	.	.	xviii

Topography . . . . Architectural descriptions compiled or
                        revised by A. P. BAGGS

Bramber Rape *(North-western Part)*	.	.	By T. P. HUDSON	.	.	1
East Easwrith Hundred	.	.	By C. R. J. CURRIE	.	.	5
Itchingfield	.	.	.	By C. R. J. CURRIE	.	.	7
Sullington	.	.	.	By C. R. J. CURRIE	.	.	18
Thakeham	.	.	.	By C. R. J. CURRIE	.	.	31
Warminghurst	.	.	.	By C. R. J. CURRIE	.	.	49

PAGE

West Grinstead Hundred . . . By T. P. HUDSON 61
   Ashington . . . . . By T. P. HUDSON 63
   Ashurst . . . . . By T. P. HUDSON 74
   West Grinstead . . . . By T. P. HUDSON 83
   Shipley . . . . . By T. P. HUDSON 105
Singlecross Hundred *(Part)* . . By T. P. HUDSON 128
   Horsham . . . . . By T. P. HUDSON 129
   Warnham . . . . . By T. P. HUDSON 203
Index 219

VOLUME SIX, PART THREE
Bramber Rape (North-eastern Part), including Crawley New Town
Edited by T. P. Hudson
(1987)

PAGE

Dedication v
Contents ix
List of Illustrations x
List of Maps xii
Editorial Note xiii
Classes of Documents in the Public Record Office xv
Classes of Documents in the Sussex Record Offices xvi
Sussex Record Society Volumes xvii
Note on Abbreviations xix
Topography . . . . . Architectural descriptions compiled or
                         revised by A. P. BAGGS

   Bramber Rape *(North-eastern Part)* . . By T. P. HUDSON . . . 1
   Burbeach Hundred . . . By T. P. HUDSON . . . 5
      Lower Beeding . . . . By T. P. HUDSON . . . 7
      Upper Beeding . . . . By T. P. HUDSON . . . 29
      Edburton . . . . By T. P. HUDSON . . . 45
      Ifield . . . . By T. P. HUDSON . . . 53
   Crawley New Town . . . By C. R. J. CURRIE . . . 74
   Singlecross Hundred *(continued)* 97
      Nuthurst . . . . By T. P. HUDSON . . . 97
      Rusper . . . . By T. P. HUDSON . . . 109
   Tipnoak Hundred . . . . By T. P. HUDSON . . . 120
      Albourne . . . . By T. P. HUDSON . . . 123
      Henfield . . . . By T. P. HUDSON . . . 133
      Woodmancote . . . . By T. P. HUDSON . . . 158
   Wyndham Half-Hundred . . . By C. R. ELRINGTON . . . 169
      Cowfold . . . . By C. R. ELRINGTON . . . 171
      Shermanbury . . . . By C. R. ELRINGTON . . . 189
Index . . . . . By C. R. J. CURRIE . . . 199
Corrigenda to Volumes I and VI (Parts 1 and 2) and to Index to Volumes I–IV, VII, and IX . 222

INDEX TO VOLUMES I–IV, VII, AND IX
Edited by Susan M. Keeling and C. P. Lewis;
compiled by D. W. Hutchings, L. J. Johnson, Jennifer Leslie, K. C. Leslie,
Monica Maloney, and A. R. Rumble
(1984)

WILTSHIRE

VOLUME ONE, PART TWO
Edited by Elizabeth Crittall
(1973)

		PAGE
Dedication		v
Contents		ix
List of Plates		x
List of Figures in the Text		xi
Editorial Note		xiii
Wiltshire Victoria County History Committee		xiv
Note on Editorial Method and Abbreviations		xv
The Beginnings of Human Settlement: Palaeolithic and Mesolithic Periods, to c. 4000 B.C.	By Stuart Piggott, C.B.E., F.B.A.	281
The First Agricultural Communities: Neolithic Period, c. 3000–1500 B.C.	By Stuart Piggott, C.B.E., F.B.A.	284
The Later Neolithic: Single-Graves and the First Metallurgy, c. 2000–c. 1500 B.C.	By Stuart Piggott, C.B.E., F.B.A.	333
The Wessex Culture of the Early Bronze Age	By Stuart Piggott, C.B.E., F.B.A.	352
The Final Phase of Bronze Technology, c. 1500–c. 500 B.C.	By Stuart Piggott, C.B.E., F.B.A.	376
The Early Pre-Roman Iron Age, c. 650–c. 400 B.C.	By B. W. Cunliffe	408
The Middle Pre-Roman Iron Age, c. 400–c. 100 B.C.	By B. W. Cunliffe	417
The Late Pre-Roman Iron Age, c. 100 B.C.–A.D. 43	By B. W. Cunliffe	426
The Period of Romanization, 43–c. 250	By B. W. Cunliffe	439
The Later Roman Period, c. 250–367	By B. W. Cunliffe	453
The End of the Roman Era, 367–500	By B. W. Cunliffe	460
The Pagan Saxon Period, c. 500–c. 700	By D. J. Bonney	468
Index	By Elizabeth Crittall	485

VOLUME TEN
Edited by Elizabeth Crittall
(1975)

		PAGE
Dedication		v
Contents		ix
List of Illustrations		x
List of Maps and Plans		xii
Editorial Note		xiii
Wiltshire Victoria County History Committee		xiv
Classes of Documents in the Public Record Office used		xv
Note on Abbreviations		xvii
Publications of the Wiltshire Record Society used		xix
Topography	Architectural descriptions prepared in collaboration with Margaret Tomlinson and A. P. Baggs	
Swanborough Hundred	By Elizabeth Crittall	1
Alton Barnes	By D. A. Crowley	8
Beechingstoke	By Janet H. Stevenson	14
All Cannings	By D. A. Crowley	20
Charlton	By Janet H. Stevenson	33
Great Cheverell	By Janet H. Stevenson	41
Little Cheverell	By D. A. Crowley	53

		PAGE
Chirton	By Janet H. Stevenson . .	60
Etchilhampton	By D. A. Crowley . .	71
Huish	By D. A. Crowley . .	77
Market Lavington . . .	By Elizabeth Crittall . .	82
Manningford Abbots . . .	By Janet H. Stevenson . .	106
Manningford Bruce . . .	By Janet H. Stevenson . .	113
Marden	By Janet H. Stevenson . .	119
North Newnton . . .	By D. A. Crowley . .	126
Rushall	By D. A. Crowley . .	136
Stanton St. Bernard . . .	By D. A. Crowley . .	146
Stert	By Elizabeth Crittall . .	155
Upavon	By D. A. Crowley . .	159
Urchfont	By Janet H. Stevenson . .	173
Wilcot	By D. A. Crowley . .	196
Wilsford	By Janet H. Stevenson . .	204
Woodborough	By D. A. Crowley . .	214
The Borough of Devizes . . .	By Ralph B. Pugh, d.lit. .	225
Index	By Elizabeth Crittall . .	315
Corrigenda to Volumes I–IX		347

VOLUME ELEVEN
Downton Hundred, Elstub and Everleigh Hundred
Edited by D. A. Crowley
(1980)

		PAGE
Dedication		v
Contents		ix
List of Illustrations		xi
List of Maps		xiii
Editorial Note		xv
Wiltshire Victoria County History Committee		xvi
Classes of Documents in the Public Record Office used . . .		xvii
Note on Abbreviations		xviii
Topography	Architectural investigation by A. P. Baggs	
Downton Hundred . . .	By D. A. Crowley . .	1
Bishopstone	By D. A. Crowley . .	3
Downton	By D. A. Crowley . .	19
Barford		52
Charlton		55
Hamptworth . . .		59
Nunton and Bodenham . .		62
Standlynch . . .		68
Wick		72
Witherington . . .		75
Fonthill Bishop . . .	By D. A. Crowley . .	77
East Knoyle . . .	By D. A. Crowley . .	82
Hindon		98
Elstub and Everleigh Hundred . .	By Janet H. Stevenson . .	105
Collingbourne Ducis . .	By Elizabeth Crittall . .	108
Enford	By Janet H. Stevenson . .	115
Everleigh	By Elizabeth Crittall . .	135
Fittleton	By Elizabeth Crittall . .	142
Ham	By Janet H. Stevenson . .	151
Little Hinton . . .	By Janet H. Stevenson . .	159
Netheravon . . .	By Janet H. Stevenson . .	165

		PAGE
Overton	By Janet H. Stevenson	181
Patney	By Janet H. Stevenson	203
Rollestone	By Jane Freeman	208
Stockton	By D. A. Crowley	212
Westwood	By Janet H. Stevenson	223
Wroughton	By Elizabeth Crittall	235
Index	By D. A. Crowley	253

VOLUME TWELVE

Ramsbury Hundred, Selkley Hundred, The Borough of Marlborough

Edited by D. A. Crowley

(1983)

		PAGE
Dedication		v
Contents		ix
List of Illustrations		xi
List of Maps and Plans		xiii
Editorial Note		xv
Wiltshire Victoria County History Committee		xvi
Classes of Documents in the Public Record Office used		xvii
Note on Abbreviations		xix
Topography	Architectural investigation by A. P. Baggs	
Ramsbury Hundred	By D. A. Crowley	1
Bishopstone	By D. A. Crowley	3
Ramsbury	By D. A. Crowley	12
Axford		47
Baydon		52
Selkley Hundred	By Janet H. Stevenson	62
Aldbourne	By Jane Freeman	67
Avebury	By Jane Freeman	86
Broad Hinton	By Jane Freeman	105
East Kennett	By Jane Freeman	119
Mildenhall	By Jane Freeman	125
Ogbourne St. Andrew	By Jane Freeman	138
Ogbourne St. George	By Jane Freeman	151
Preshute	By Janet H. Stevenson	160
Winterbourne Bassett	By Jane Freeman	184
Winterbourne Monkton	By Jane Freeman	192
The Borough of Marlborough	By Janet H. Stevenson	199
Index	By Janet H. Stevenson	230

VOLUME THIRTEEN

South-West Wiltshire: Chalke and Dunworth Hundreds

Edited by D. A. Crowley

(1987)

	PAGE
Dedication	v
Contents	ix
List of Illustrations	xi
List of Maps	xiii
Editorial Note	xv
Wiltshire Victoria County History Committee	xvi
Classes of Documents in the Public Record Office used	xvii
Note on Abbreviations	xix

PAGE

Topography	Architectural investigation by A. P. BAGGS	
Introduction	By D. A. CROWLEY	1
Chalke Hundred	By JANE FREEMAN	3
Alvediston	By JANE FREEMAN	7
Berwick St. John	By JANE FREEMAN	16
Bower Chalke	By JANE FREEMAN	29
Broad Chalke	By JANE FREEMAN	37
Ebbesborne Wake	By JANE FREEMAN	52
Fifield Bavant	By JANE FREEMAN	60
Semley	By JANE FREEMAN	66
Tollard Royal	By JANE FREEMAN	79
Dunworth Hundred	By JANET H. STEVENSON	89
Ansty	By JANET H. STEVENSON	93
Berwick St. Leonard	By D. A. CROWLEY	100
Chicklade	By D. A. CROWLEY	105
Chilmark	By D. A. CROWLEY	114
Donhead St. Andrew	By JANET H. STEVENSON	126
Donhead St. Mary	By JANET H. STEVENSON	138
Fonthill Gifford	By D. A. CROWLEY	155
Sedgehill	By JANET H. STEVENSON	169
Swallowcliffe	By JANET H. STEVENSON	177
Teffont Evias	By JANET H. STEVENSON	185
Tisbury	By D. A. CROWLEY	195
Index	By JANET H. STEVENSON	249
Corrigenda to Volumes I–XII		278

YORKSHIRE, EAST RIDING

VOLUME TWO

Edited by K. J. Allison

(1974)

PAGE

Dedication	v
Contents	ix
List of Illustrations	x
List of Maps and Plans	xii
Editorial Note	xiii
Classes of Documents in the Public Record Office used	xiv
Note on Abbreviations	xv

Topography	Descriptions of buildings by MARGARET TOMLINSON	
Dickering Wapentake	By K. J. ALLISON and J. D. PURDY	1
Argam	By K. J. ALLISON	6
Bempton	By J. D. PURDY	8
Bessingby	By J. D. PURDY	16
Boynton	By J. D. PURDY	21
Bridlington	By K. J. ALLISON	29
Burton Agnes	By K. J. ALLISON	106
Burton Fleming	By K. J. ALLISON	119
Carnaby	By J. D. PURDY	125
Filey	By K. J. ALLISON	131
Flamborough	By J. D. PURDY	151
Folkton	By J. D. PURDY	164
Foston on the Wolds	By K. J. ALLISON	176

PAGE

Foxholes	By J. D. PURDY		190
Fraisthorpe	By J. D. PURDY		199
Ganton	By J. D. PURDY		208
Garton on the Wolds	By J. D. PURDY		216
Harpham	By K. J. ALLISON		223
Hunmanby	By K. J. ALLISON		228
Little Kelk	By K. J. ALLISON		245
Kilham	By J. D. PURDY		247
Langtoft	By J. D. PURDY		263
Lowthorpe	By K. J. ALLISON		271
Muston	By K. J. ALLISON		278
Nafferton	By K. J. ALLISON		283
Wold Newton	By K. J. ALLISON		297
Reighton	By K. J. ALLISON		303
Rudston	By J. D. PURDY		310
Ruston Parva	By K. J. ALLISON		320
Thwing	By K. J. ALLISON		324
Willerby	By K. J. ALLISON		332
Index	By K. J. ALLISON		340
Corrigenda to Volume I			365

VOLUME THREE

Edited by K. J. Allison

(1976)

PAGE

Dedication			v
Contents			ix
List of Illustrations			x
List of Maps and Plans			xii
Editorial Note			xiii
Classes of Documents in the Public Record Office used			xiv
Note on Abbreviations			xv
Topography	Architectural investigation by A. P. BAGGS		
Ouse and Derwent Wapentake	By K. J. ALLISON		1
Dunnington	By J. D. PURDY		5
Elvington	By J. D. PURDY		12
Escrick	By K. J. ALLISON		17
Fulford	By K. J. ALLISON		29
Hemingbrough	By K. J. ALLISON		37
Hemingbrough			37
Barlby			47
Brackenholme with Woodhall			52
Cliffe with Lund			55
South Duffield			60
Menthorpe with Bowthorpe			63
Osgodby			64
Heslington	By K. J. ALLISON		66
Naburn	By K. J. ALLISON		74
Riccall	By K. J. ALLISON		82
Skipwith	By K. J. ALLISON		89
Stillingfleet	By J. D. PURDY		101
Thorganby	By J. D. PURDY		112
Wheldrake	By K. J. ALLISON		120
Harthill Wapentake	By K. J. ALLISON		129
Wilton Beacon division (western part)			
Allerthorpe	By G. H. R. KENT		133

PAGE

Barmby Moor . . . . . By G. H. R. Kent . . . 140
Catton . . . . . By K. J. Allison 147
   High and Low Catton and Stamford Bridge East 147
   Kexby, Scoreby, and Stamford Bridge West 158
Fangfoss . . . . . By G. H. R. Kent . . . 164
Full Sutton . . . . . By K. J. Allison 170
Sutton upon Derwent . . . By K. J. Allison 173
Thornton . . . . . By G. H. R. Kent . . . 179
Wilberfoss . . . . . By K. J. Allison 190
Index . . . . . . By K. J. Allison and G. H. R. Kent . 198

VOLUME FOUR
Edited by K. J. Allison
(1979)

PAGE

Dedication v
Contents ix
List of Illustrations x
List of Maps and Plans xii
Editorial Note xiii
Classes of Documents in the Public Record Office used xiv
Note on Abbreviations xv
Topography . . . . . Architectural investigation by A. P. Baggs
   Harthill Wapentake, Hunsley Beacon division . By K. J. Allison 1
   Bishop Burton . . . . By K. J. Allison 3
   Cherry Burton . . . . By K. J. Allison 11
   North Cave . . . . By G. H. R. Kent . . . 19
   South Cave . . . . By K. J. Allison 37
   Cottingham . . . . By K. J. Allison 61
   South Dalton . . . . By G. H. R. Kent . . . 85
   Elloughton . . . . By K. J. Allison 93
   Etton . . . . . By G. H. R. Kent . . . 103
   Hotham . . . . . By G. H. R. Kent . . . 115
   Leconfield . . . . By G. H. R. Kent . . . 123
   Newbald . . . . . By K. J. Allison 131
   Rowley . . . . . By K. J. Allison 140
   Sancton . . . . . By K. J. Allison 155
   Skidby . . . . . By G. H. R. Kent . . . 164
Index . . . . . By G. H. R. Kent . . . 173
Corrigenda to Volumes I, II, and III 187

VOLUME FIVE
Holderness: Southern Part
Edited by K. J. Allison
(1984)

PAGE

Dedication v
Contents ix
List of Illustrations x
List of Maps xii
Editorial Note xiii
Classes of Documents in the Public Record Office xiv
Note on Abbreviations xv
Topography . . . . . Architectural investigation by A. P. Baggs

		PAGE
Holderness Wapentake	By K. J. ALLISON	1
South division		
Burstwick	By G. H. R. KENT . . .	7
Easington	By K. J. ALLISON	21
Halsham	By G. H. R. KENT . . .	31
Hollym	By K. J. ALLISON	40
Holmpton	By K. J. ALLISON	47
Keyingham	By G. H. R. KENT . . .	55
Kilnsea	By K. J. ALLISON	65
Ottringham	By G. H. R. KENT . . .	74
Owthorne	By K. J. ALLISON	85
Patrington	By K. J. ALLISON	97
Paull	By G. H. R. KENT . . .	111
Skeffling	By K. J. ALLISON	127
Sunk Island	By K. J. ALLISON	135
Welwick	By K. J. ALLISON	139
Winestead	By G. H. R. KENT . . .	148
Withernsea	By K. J. ALLISON	157
Middle division (part of)		
Hedon	By K. J. ALLISON	168
Preston	By G. H. R. KENT . . .	186
Index		203
Corrigenda to Volumes I–IV		223

VOLUME SIX
The Borough and Liberties of Beverley
Edited by K. J. Allison
(1989)

		PAGE
Dedication		v
Contents		ix
List of Illustrations		xi
List of Maps, Plans, and Figures		xii
Editorial Note		xiii
Classes of Documents in the Public Record Office		xiv
Note on Abbreviations		xv
The Borough and Liberties of Beverley . .	Architectural descriptions written or revised by A. P. BAGGS	
Introduction	By K. J. ALLISON	1
Medieval Beverley	By R. E. HORROX	2
Beverley and St. John		2
The Archbishop and Beverley		11
The Chapter and Beverley		16
Local Government		19
Town Finance		30
Trade and Industry		34
The Guilds and their Plays		42
Topography and Growth		49
The Townspeople		57
Beverley in the 16th Century . . .	The sections on the Achievement of Self-government, Town Government, Economy, and Population and Topography are by K. J. ALLISON, the rest by G. H. R. KENT . .	63
The Achievement of Self-government		63
Town Government		65

CONTENTS OF VOLUMES: YORKS. E.R. VI

PAGE

Political Affairs before 1542 70
Political Affairs after 1542 73
Parliamentary Representation 75
Religious Life 76
Economy 80
Population and Topography 83
Beverley in the 17th Century . . . By G. C. F. Forster . . . 89
Religious Life to 1642 89
Parliamentary Representation to 1640 90
Military and Political Affairs, 1642–60 91
Religious Life after 1642 95
Parliamentary Representation and Politics after 1660 97
The Charters and Town Government 100
Economy 105
Population and Topography 107
Beverley, 1700–1835 . . . . By David Neave . . . 112
Economy 112
Population and Topography 118
Town Government 121
Parliamentary Elections 126
Social Life and Conditions 131
Modern Beverley . . . . . By Lucy M. Brown . . . 136
Economy, 1835–1918 136
Political and Social History, 1835–1918 141
Religious and Cultural Life, 1835–1918 148
Beverley, 1918–45 151
Beverley after 1945 154
Boundaries . . . . . By K. J. Allison . . . 161
Communications . . . . . By K. J. Allison . . . 164
Street Names . . . . . By K. J. Allison . . . 169
Fortifications . . . . . By G. H. R. Kent . . . 178
Sites and Remains of Religious Houses . . By K. J. Allison . . . 180
Secular Buildings . . . . . By Ivan Hall . . . 183
Public Institutions . . . . . By K. J. Allison . . . 190
The Arms, Seals, Insignia, and Plate of the Town . By G. H. R. Kent . . . 195
Lists of Officers . . . . . By K. J. Allison . . . 198
Social Institutions . . . . . By K. J. Allison . . . 206
Manors . . . . . . By K. J. Allison . . . 210
Common Lands . . . . . By K. J. Allison . . . 211
Markets and Fairs . . . . . By K. J. Allison . . . 218
Public Services . . . . . By K. J. Allison . . . 223
Churches . . . . . By K. J. Allison . . . 231
Roman Catholicism . . . . By G. H. R. Kent . . . 242
Protestant Nonconformity . . . . By G. H. R. Kent . . . 242
Education . . . . . By G. H. R. Kent . . . 250
Charities . . . . . . By K. J. Allison . . . 261
Outlying Townships
Beverley Parks . . . . . By K. J. Allison . . . 271
Eske . . . . . . By K. J. Allison . . . 278
Molescroft . . . . . By G. H. R. Kent . . . 281
Storkhill and Sandholme . . . By G. H. R. Kent . . . 291
Thearne and Woodmansey . . . By K. J. Allison . . . 295
Tickton . . . . . By G. H. R. Kent . . . 301
Weel . . . . . . By G. H. R. Kent . . . 308
Index . . . . . By K. J. Allison and G. H. R. Kent . 315
Corrigenda to Volumes III, IV, and V 337

INDEX OF TITLES OF ARTICLES

THE following index is of the titles of articles that are printed in the tables of contents. All the places other than the counties themselves that are named in the tables are indexed, apart from that for the *Essex* Bibliography Supplement. Where, however, the tables list the sections of general articles or the topical or chronological sections of topographical articles the titles of those sections are not necessarily indexed. No attempt has been made to index contents that are not listed in the tables of contents, and the index therefore contains no references to subjects that may be treated extensively in the volumes concerned, for example Architecture or Buildings in the topographical volumes. Where a table of contents lists more than one religious house or more than one school in a single place the titles of the several houses or schools have not been itemized, and are collectively indexed under the headings 'religious houses' and 'schools'.

Abington, Great and Little, *Cambs.* vi
Abington Pigotts, *Cambs.* viii
Acton, *Mdx.* vii
Acton Grammar School, *Ches.* iii
Administrative History, *Ches.* ii; *and see* Government
Agriculture, *Mdx.* ix; *Salop.* iv; *Staffs.* vi; Agrarian Economy and Domesday Settlement, *Ches.* i; Early Agriculturalists, *Ches.* i; First Agricultural Communities, *Wilts.* i (2); Roman, *Cambs.* vii
Alberbury Priory, *Salop.* ii
Aldermen 1483–1835, List of, *Glos.* iv
Albourne, *Suss.* vi (3)
Aldbourne, *Wilts.* xii
Aldsworth, *Glos.* vii
Aller, *Som.* iii
Allerthorpe, *Yorks. E.R.* iii
Alton Barnes, *Wilts.* x
Alvediston, *Wilts.* xiii
Amblecote, *Staffs.* xx
Anglo-Saxon (Saxon) period, *Ches.* i; *Wilts.* i (2)
Anglo-Saxon Ecclesiastical Centre, *Staffs.* xiv
Ansty, *Wilts.* xiii
Argam, *Yorks. E.R.* ii
Armingford Hundred, *Cambs.* viii
Arms, Seals, Insignia, and Plate, *Glos.* iv; *Oxon.* iv; *Yorks. E.R.* vi; *and see* Officers
Arrington, *Cambs.* v
Art and Artefacts, Anglo-Saxon, *Ches.* i
Ashington, *Suss.* vi (2)
Ashurst, *Suss.* vi (2)
Assarting, *Salop.* iv
Assessments, *see* Tax Assessments
Aston, North, *Oxon.* xi
Aston, Steeple, *Oxon.* xi
Athletics, *Salop.* ii
Audlem Grammar School, *Ches.* iii
Avebury, *Wilts.* xii
Aveley, *Essex* viii
Avening, *Glos.* xi
Axford (in Ramsbury), *Wilts.* xii

Babraham, *Cambs.* vi
Bailiffs 1200–1483, List of, *Glos.* iv

Balsham, *Cambs.* vi
Banbury, *Oxon.* x; Hundred, *Oxon.* x
Barford (in Downton), *Wilts.* xi
Barford St. Michael, *Oxon.* xi
Barlby (in Hemingbrough), *Yorks. E.R.* iii
Barmby Moor, *Yorks E.R.* iii
Barnet, Friern, *Mdx.* vi
Barnsley, *Glos.* vii
Barnwood, *Glos.* iv
Barrington, *Cambs.* v
Barrington, *Som.* iv
Bartlow, *Cambs.* vi
Barton, *Cambs.* v
Barton, Steeple, *Oxon.* xi
Barton, Westcott, *Oxon.* xi
Bassingbourn, *Cambs.* viii
Battlefield, College of St. Mary Magdalen, *Salop.* ii
Baydon (in Ramsbury), *Wilts.* xii
Bayswater (in Paddington), *Mdx.* ix
Becontree Hundred [part], *Essex* vi
Beechingstoke, *Wilts.* x
Beeding, Lower and Upper, *Suss.* vi (3)
Begbroke, *Oxon.* xii
Belsize (in Hampstead), *Mdx.* ix
Bempton, *Yorks. E.R.* ii
Berwick St. John, *Wilts.* xiii
Berwick St. Leonard, *Wilts.* xiii
Bessingby, *Yorks. E.R.* ii
Beverley, Borough and Liberties, *Yorks. E.R.* vi; Beverley Parks, *Yorks. E.R.* vi
Bibliography, *Essex* Bibl. Supp.
Bibury, *Glos.* vii
Bicknoller, *Som.* v
Birkenhead: Priory, *Ches.* iii; School, *Ches.* iii
Bishopstone (in Downton Hundred), *Wilts.* xi
Bishopstone (in Ramsbury Hundred), *Wilts.* xii
Bisley, *Glos.* xi; Hundred, *Glos.* xi
Bitterley Grammar School, *Salop.* ii
Bladon, *Oxon.* xii
Blaisdon, *Glos.* x
Blenheim (in Woodstock), *Oxon.* xii
Bobbington, *Staffs.* xx
Bodenham (in Downton, with Nunton), *Wilts.* xi

Boroughs, Domesday, *Ches.* i
Botolphs, *Suss.* vi (1)
Bourn, *Cambs.* v
Bourton, Great and Little (in Cropredy), *Oxon.* x
Bowthorpe (in Menthorpe in Hemingbrough), *Yorks. E.R.* iii
Boxworth, *Cambs.* ix
Boynton, *Yorks. E.R.* ii
Brackenholme, with Woodhall (in Hemingbrough), *Yorks. E.R.* iii
Bradford Hundred, Southern Division (part), *Salop.* xi
Bramber, *Suss.* vi (1); Rape, *Suss.* vi (1)–(3)
Brentford (with Ealing), *Mdx.* vii
Brentwood (with South Weald), *Essex* viii
Brewood: Grammar School, *Staffs.* vi; Priory of St. Leonard, *Salop.* ii
Bridgnorth: Grammar School, *Salop.* ii; religious houses, *Salop.* ii
Bridlington, *Yorks. E.R.* ii
Brightford Hundred, *Suss.* vi (1)
Brightwells Barrow Hundred, *Glos.* vii
Brimpsfield, *Glos.* vii
Brinkley, *Cambs.* vi
Broadwater, *Suss.* vi (1)
Bromfield Priory, *Salop.* ii
Bromley, Abbots, School of St. Mary and St. Anne, *Staffs.* vi
Brompton Ralph, *Som.* v
Bromwich, West, *Staffs.* xvii
Bronze Age, *Ches* i; *Wilts.* i (2)
Buddhism, *Mdx.* ix
Buildings, Anglo-Saxon, *Ches.* i
Buildwas Abbey, *Salop.* ii
Bull-Baiting, *see* Cock-Fighting
Bunbury Grammar School, *Ches.* iii
Burbeach Hundred, *Suss.* vi (3)
Burial, Roman, *see* Religion
Burntwood (in Lichfield), *Staffs.* xiv
Burrough Green, *Cambs.* vi
Burstwick, *Yorks. E.R.* v
Burton, Bishop, *Yorks. E.R.* iv
Burton, Cherry, *Yorks. E.R.* iv
Burton Agnes, *Yorks. E.R.* ii
Burton Fleming, *Yorks. E.R.* ii
Burton-upon-Trent Grammar School, *Staffs.* vi

Calday Grange Grammar School, *see* Kirby, West
Caldecote, *Cambs.* v
Camel, West, *Som.* iii
Camps, Castle, *Cambs.* vi
Camps, Shudy, *Cambs.* vi
Cannings, All, *Wilts.* x
Careswell Foundation, *Salop.* ii
Carlton cum Willingham, *Cambs.* vi
Carnaby, *Yorks. E.R.* ii
Cassington, *Oxon.* xii
Catton, *Yorks. E.R.* iii; High and Low Catton, and Stamford Bridge East, *Yorks. E.R.* iii
Cave, North and South, *Yorks. E.R.* iv
Caxton, *Cambs.* v
Cerney, North, *Glos.* vii
Chaffcombe, *Som.* iv
Chafford Hundred, *Essex* vii–viii
Chalcots (in Hampstead), *Mdx.* ix

Chalke, Bower, *Wilts.* xiii
Chalke, Broad, *Wilts.* xiii
Chalke Hundred, *Wilts.* xiii
Charlbury, *Oxon.* x
Charlton (in Downton, and in Downton Hundred), *Wilts.* xi
Charlton (in Swanborough Hundred), *Wilts.* x
Charlton Adam, *Som.* iii
Charlton Mackrell, *Som.* iii
Charters and Town Government, *Yorks. E.R.* vi
Chedworth, *Glos.* vii
Cherington, *Glos.* xi
Cheshire and North-East Wales under the Mercian Kings, *Ches.* i
Chester: Cathedral, *Ches.* iii; Diocese, *Ches.* iii; Earldom, *Ches.* ii; Palatinate, *Ches.* ii; Parliamentary Representation, *Ches.* ii; religious houses, *Ches.* iii; Roman, *Ches.* i; schools, *Ches.* iii
Chesterton, *Cambs.* ix; Hundred, *Cambs.* ix
Cheverell, Great and Little, *Wilts.* x
Chicklade, *Wilts.* xiii
Childerditch, *Essex* viii
Childerley, *Cambs.* ix
Childs Hill (in Hampstead), *Mdx.* ix
Chilford Hundred, *Cambs.* vi
Chillington, *Som.* iv
Chilmark, *Wilts.* xiii
Chipstable, *Som.* v
Chirbury Priory, *Salop.* ii
Chirton, *Wilts.* x
Chiswick, *Mdx.* vii
Church, The, *see* Ecclesiastical Organization
Churcham, *Glos.* x
City Government, *see* Government
Clapham, *Suss.* vi (1)
Clattercote (in Cropredy), *Oxon.* x
Clatworthy, *Som.* v
Claydon (in Cropredy), *Oxon.* x
Cleeve, Old, *Som.* v
Cliffe, with Lund (in Hemingbrough), *Yorks. E.R.* iii
Clopton (in Croydon), *Cambs.* viii
Coalbrookdale (in Madeley), *Salop.* xi
Coalport (in Madeley), *Salop.* xi
Coberley, *Glos.* vii
Cock-Fighting and Bull-Baiting, *Salop.* ii
Codsall, *Staffs.* xx
Cogges, *Oxon.* xii
Colesbourne, *Glos.* vii
Collingbourne Ducis, *Wilts.* xi
Coln St. Aldwyns, *Glos.* vii
Combe, *Oxon.* xii
Combermere Abbey, *Ches.* iii
Comberton, *Cambs.* v
Commons, *Salop.* iv
Conington, *Cambs.* ix
Coombes, *Suss.* vi (1)
Corrigenda, *Cambs.* v–vi, viii–ix; *Essex* vi, Bibl. Supp.; *Glos.* x–xi; *Mdx.* iv–ix; *Salop.* ii–iv, xi; *Suss.* vi (3), Index; *Wilts.* x, xiii; *Yorks. E.R.* ii, iv–vi
Coton, *Cambs.* v
Cottenham, *Cambs.* ix
Cottingham, *Yorks. E.R.* iv
Cotton College, formerly Sedgley Park School, *Staffs.* vi
County Councils 1889–1974, *Ches.* ii; *Salop.* iii

INDEX OF TITLES OF ARTICLES

County Government, *see* Government
Coursing, *Salop.* ii
Cowfold, *Suss.* vi (3)
Cowley, *Glos.* vii
Cranham, *Essex* vii
Cranham, *Glos.* vii
Crawley New Town, *Suss.* vi (3)
Crewkerne, *Som.* iv; Hundred, *Som.* iv
Cricket, *Cambs.* v; *Salop.* ii
Cricket St. Thomas, *Som.* iv
Cricklewood (in Hampstead, with Kilburn and Edgware Road), *Mdx.* ix
Cropredy, *Oxon.* x
Crowcombe, *Som.* v
Croxton, *Cambs.* v
Croydon cum Clopton, *Cambs.* viii
Cudworth, *Som.* iv
Cultural Life, *see* Religious and Cultural Life; Social and Cultural Activities
Curborough and Elmhurst (in Lichfield), *Staffs.* xiv
Currency, Roman, *Cambs.* vii

Dalton, South, *Yorks. E.R.* iv
Dawley, *Salop.* xi
Deddington, *Oxon.* xi
Denhall, Hospital of St. Andrew, *Ches.* iii
Denstone College, *Staffs.* vi
Deva, *Ches.* i
Devizes, Borough, *Wilts.* x
Dickering Wapentake, *Yorks. E.R.* ii
Dinnington, *Som.* iv
Dodington, *Som.* v
Domesday Book: Introduction and Translation, *Ches.* i; Indexes: *Ches.* i; *Salop.* ii
Donhead St. Andrew, *Wilts.* xiii
Donhead St. Mary, *Wilts.* xiii
Donnington, formerly Wroxeter, Grammar School, *Salop.* ii
Dowlish Wake, *Som.* iv
Downton, *Wilts.* xi; Hundred, *Wilts.* xi
Drayton, Dry, *Cambs.* ix
Drayton, Fen, *Cambs.* ix
Drayton, Market, Grammar School, *Salop.* ii
Duffield, South, *Yorks. E.R.* iii
Dullingham, *Cambs.* vi
Dunnington, *Yorks. E.R.* iii
Dunworth Hundred, *Wilts.* xiii
Durrington, *Suss.* vi (1)
Duxford, *Cambs.* vi

Ealing and Brentford, *Mdx.* vii
Easington, *Yorks. E.R.* v
Eastington, *Glos.* x
Eastleach Martin, *Glos.* vii
Eastleach Turville, *Glos.* vii
Easwrith, East, Hundred, *Suss.* vi (2)
Ebbesborne Wake, *Wilts.* xiii
Ecclesiastical Organization, *Salop.* ii; Anglo-Saxon Church, *Ches.* i; The Church before the Reformation, *Ches.* iii
Edburton, *Suss.* vi (3)
Edgeworth, *Glos.* xi
Edgware, *Mdx.* iv
Edgware Road (in Hampstead, with Kilburn and Cricklewood), *Mdx.* ix

Edmonton, *Mdx.* v; Hundred, *Mdx.* v
Education: Agricultural, *Salop.* iv; Education before 1903, *Ches.* iii; *and see* Keele University; Schools
Elkstone, *Glos.* vii
Ellesmere College, *Salop.* ii
Elloughton, *Yorks. E.R.* iv
Elmhurst (in Lichfield, with Curborough), *Staffs.* xiv
Elstub and Everleigh Hundred, *Wilts.* xi
Elsworth, *Cambs.* ix
Elthorne Hundred [part], *Mdx.* iv
Eltisley, *Cambs.* v
Elvington, *Yorks. E.R.* iii
Elworthy, *Som.* v
Enfield, *Mdx.* v
Enford, *Wilts.* xi
Enville, *Staffs.* xx
Ercall, High, Grammar School, *Salop.* ii
Escrick, *Yorks. E.R.* iii
Eske (in Beverley), *Yorks. E.R.* vi
Etchilhampton, *Wilts.* x
Etton, *Yorks. E.R.* iv
Everleigh, *Wilts.* xi; Hundred, *see* Elstub
Eversden, Great and Little, *Cambs.* v
Eynsham, *Oxon.* xii
Eyton upon the Weald Moors, *Salop.* xi

Fairford, *Glos.* vii
Fangfoss, *Yorks. E.R.* iii
Farming, *see* Agriculture
Fifield Bavant, *Wilts.* xiii
Filey, *Yorks. E.R.* ii
Finchley, *Mdx.* vi
Findon, *Suss.* vi (1)
Fishersgate Half-Hundred, *Suss.* vi (1)
Fisherwick, with Tamhorn (in Lichfield), *Staffs.* xiv
Fishing (sport), *Cambs.* v; *Salop.* ii
Fittleton, *Wilts.* xi
Flamborough, *Yorks. E.R.* ii
Folkton, *Yorks. E.R.* ii
Fonthill Bishop, *Wilts.* xi
Fonthill Gifford, *Wilts.* xiii
Football, *Cambs.* v; Association, *Salop.* ii
Forests, *Ches.* ii
Foston on the Wolds, *Yorks. E.R.* ii
Fowlmere, *Cambs.* viii
Fox-Hunting, *Cambs.* v; *Salop.* ii
Foxholes, *Yorks. E.R.* ii
Foxton, *Cambs.* viii
Fraisthorpe, *Yorks. E.R.* ii
Frampton on Severn, *Glos.* x
Franchises, *Salop.* iii
Freeford (in Lichfield), *Staffs.* xiv
Freemanors Hundred, *see* Williton
Fretherne and Saul, *Glos.* x
Frocester, *Glos.* x
Frognal (in Hampstead), *Mdx.* ix
Fulford, *Yorks. E.R.* iii

Gamlingay, *Cambs.* v
Ganton, *Yorks. E.R.* ii
Garton on the Wolds, *Yorks. E.R.* ii
Geology, *Ches.* i
Girton, *Cambs.* ix
Gloucester: City, *Glos.* iv; Castle, *Glos.* iv; Cathedral and the Close, *Glos.* iv

Glympton, *Oxon.* xi
Gore Hundred, *Mdx.* iv–v
Government: City, *Ches.* ii; *Glos.* iv; County, *Ches.* ii; *Salop.* iii; Town, *Glos.* iv; *Staffs.* xiv; *Yorks. E.R.* vi
Gransden, Little, *Cambs.* v
Grantchester, *Cambs.* v
Graveley, *Cambs.* ix
Greek Orthodox Church, *Mdx.* ix
Grinstead, West, *Suss.* vi (2); Hundred, *Suss.* vi (2)

Hadley, Monken, *Mdx.* v
Hadley and Horton (in Wellington), *Salop.* xi
Hallingbury, Great and Little, *Essex* viii
Halse, *Som.* v
Halsham, *Yorks. E.R.* v
Halston Preceptory, *Salop.* ii
Ham, *Wilts.* xi
Ham, East and West, *Essex* vi
Hammerwich (in Lichfield), *Staffs.* xiv
Hampstead, *Mdx.* ix; Hampstead Heath, Hampstead Town, *Mdx.* ix
Hamptworth (in Downton), *Wilts.* xi
Hanborough, *Oxon.* xii
Hardwick, *Cambs.* v
Hardwicke, *Glos.* x
Haresfield, *Glos.* x
Harlow, *Essex* viii; Hundred, *Essex* viii
Harlton, *Cambs.* v
Harmondsworth, *Mdx.* iv
Harpham, *Yorks. E.R.* ii
Harrow, including Pinner, *Mdx.* iv
Harston, *Cambs.* viii
Harthill Wapentake: Hunsley Beacon division, *Yorks. E.R.* iv; Wilton Beacon division (western part), *Yorks. E.R.* iii
Haslingfield, *Cambs.* v
Hatfield Broad Oak, *Essex* viii
Hatherop, *Glos.* vii
Hatley, East, *Cambs.* viii
Hatley St. George, *Cambs.* v
Haughmond Abbey, *Salop.* ii
Hauxton and Newton, *Cambs.* viii
Havering-atte-Bower, *Essex* vii; Liberty, *Essex* vii
Hayes, *Mdx.* iv
Hearth Tax Assessments, *see* Tax Assessments
Hedon, *Yorks. E.R.* v
Heene, *Suss.* vi (1)
Hemingbrough, *Yorks. E.R.* iii
Hempsted, *Glos.* iv
Hendon, *Mdx.* v
Henfield, *Suss.* vi (3)
Heslington, *Yorks. E.R.* iii
Heythrop, *Oxon.* xi
Highgate (in Hornsey), *Mdx.* vi
Hildersham, *Cambs.* vi
Hillingdon, including Uxbridge, *Mdx.* iv
Hindon, *Wilts.* xi
Hinton, Broad, *Wilts.* xii
Hinton, Little, *Wilts.* xi
Hinton St. George, *Som.* iv
Hinxton, *Cambs.* vi
Histon, *Cambs.* ix
Holderness Wapentake: Middle division (part), *Yorks. E.R.* v; South division, *Yorks. E.R.* v

Holford, *Som.* v
Hollym, *Yorks. E.R.* v
Holmpton, *Yorks. E.R.* v
Hornchurch, *Essex* vii
Hornsey, including Highgate, *Mdx.* vi
Horse-Racing, *Cambs.* v; *Salop.* ii
Horseheath, *Cambs.* vi
Horsham, *Suss.* vi (2)
Horsley, *Glos.* xi
Horton (in Wellington, with Hadley), *Salop.* xi
Hotham, *Yorks. E.R.* iv
Hucclecote, *Glos.* iv
Huish, *Wilts.* x
Huish Champflower, *Som.* v
Huish Episcopi, *Som.* iii
Hunmanby, *Yorks. E.R.* ii
Hunting, *see* Fox-Hunting; Otter-Hunting

Ickenham, *Mdx.* iv
Ickleton, *Cambs.* vi
Ifield, *Suss.* vi (3)
Ilchester, *Som.* iii
Ilford, Little, *Essex* vi
Impington, *Cambs.* ix
Inclosure, *Salop.* iv
Industries, Roman, *Ches.* i
Insignia, *see* Arms
Iron Age, Pre-Roman, *Wilts.* i (2)
Ironbridge (in Madeley), *Salop.* xi
Islington, *Mdx.* viii
Itchingfield, *Suss.* vi (2)

Judaism, *Mdx.* ix

Keele University, *Staffs.* vi
Kelk, Little, *Yorks. E.R.* ii
Kempsford, *Glos.* vii
Kennett, East, *Wilts.* xii
Ketley, *Salop.* xi
Kexby, Scoreby, and Stamford Bridge West (in Catton), *Yorks. E.R.* iii
Keyingham, *Yorks. E.R.* v
Kidlington, *Oxon.* xii
Kilburn, Edgware Road, and Cricklewood (in Hampstead), *Mdx.* ix
Kilham, *Yorks. E.R.* ii
Kilnsea, *Yorks. E.R.* v
Kilton, *Som.* v
Kilve, *Som.* v
Kingsbury, *Mdx.* v
Kingsbury (East) Hundred, *Som.* iii
Kingsdon, *Som.* iii
Kingston, *Cambs.* v
Kingston by Sea, *Suss.* vi (1)
Kingstone, *Som.* iii
Kinver, *Staffs.* xx
Kirby, West, Calday Grange Grammar School, *Ches.* iii
Knapwell, *Cambs.* ix
Kneesworth, *Cambs.* viii
Knowle St. Giles, *Som.* iv
Knoyle, East, *Wilts.* xi
Knutsford Grammar School, *Ches.* iii

Lancaut (in Tidenham), *Glos.* x

Lancing, *Suss.* vi (1)
Landbeach, *Cambs.* ix
Langport, *Som.* iii
Langtoft, *Yorks. E.R.* ii
Lasborough (in Westonbirt), *Glos.* xi
Latton, *Essex* viii
Lavington, Market, *Wilts.* x
Lawley (in Wellington), *Salop.* xi
Lechlade, *Glos.* vii
Leconfield, *Yorks. E.R.* iv
Leigh, North and South, *Oxon.* xii
Leyton, *Essex* vi
Lichfield: City, *Staffs.* xiv; Cathedral and Close, *Staffs.* xiv; Grammar School, *Staffs.* vi
Lilleshall, *Salop.* xi; Abbey, *Salop.* ii
Lilstock, *Som.* v
Linton, *Cambs.* vi
Litlington, *Cambs.* viii
Littleworth (in Hampstead, with North End and Spaniard's End), *Mdx.* ix
Local Authorities, New, *Ches.* ii; *Salop.* iii
Lolworth, *Cambs.* ix
Longney, *Glos.* x
Longstowe, *Cambs.* v; Hundred, *Cambs.* v
Longtree Hundred, *Glos.* xi
Lopen, *Som.* iv
Lowthorpe, *Yorks. E.R.* ii
Ludford, Hospital of St. Giles, *Salop.* ii
Ludlow: Grammar School, *Salop.* ii; religious houses, *Salop.* ii
Lund (in Cliffe in Hemingbrough), *Yorks. E.R.* iii
Lydford, East, *Som.* iii
Lydley Preceptory, *Salop.* ii
Lymm Grammar School, *Ches.* iii

Macclesfield Grammar School, *Ches.* iii
Madeley, including Coalbrookdale, Coalport, and Ironbridge, *Salop.* xi
Madingley, *Cambs.* ix
Maida Vale (in Paddington), *Mdx.* ix
Malpas Grammar School, *Ches.* iii
Manningford Abbots, *Wilts.* x
Manningford Bruce, *Wilts.* x
Marden, *Wilts.* x
Marketing, *Salop.* iv
Marlborough, Borough, *Wilts.* xii
Martock, *Som.* iv; Hundred, *Som.* iv
Matching, *Essex* viii
Matson, *Glos.* iv
Melbourn, *Cambs.* viii
Meldreth, *Cambs.* viii
Menthorpe, with Bowthorpe (in Hemingbrough), *Yorks. E.R.* iii
Mercian Kings, *see* Cheshire and North-East Wales
Merriott, *Som.* iv
Mesolithic Period, *Wilts.* i (2)
Mildenhall, *Wilts.* xii
Military Remains, Roman, *Cambs.* vii
Milton, *Cambs.* ix
Mimms, South, *Mdx.* v
Minchinhampton, *Glos.* xi
Miserden, *Glos.* xi
Misterton, *Som.* iv
Molescroft (in Beverley), *Yorks. E.R.* vi
Mollington (in Cropredy), *Oxon.* x

Monksilver, *Som.* v
Montacute, *Som.* iii
Morden, Guilden, *Cambs.* viii
Morden, Steeple, *Cambs.* viii
Moreton Valence, *Glos.* x
Morville Priory, *Salop.* ii
Mottram in Longdendale Grammar School, *Ches.* iii
Muchelney, *Som.* iii
Muston, *Yorks. E.R.* ii

Naburn, *Yorks. E.R.* iii
Nafferton, *Yorks. E.R.* ii
Nailsworth, *Glos.* xi
Nantwich: Grammar School, *Ches.* iii; religious houses, *Ches.* iii
Neolithic Period, *Wilts.* i (2)
Netheravon, *Wilts.* xi
Netteswell, *Essex* viii
Nettlecombe, *Som.* v
Newbald, *Yorks. E.R.* iv
Newcastle-under-Lyme Grammar School, *Staffs.* vi
Newington, South, *Oxon.* xi
Newnham, *Glos.* x
Newnton, North, *Wilts.* x
Newport: Adams' Grammar School, *Salop.* ii; religious houses, *Salop.* ii
Newton, with Hauxton, *Cambs.* viii
Newton, Wold, *Yorks. E.R.* ii
Nonconformity, *see* Protestant Nonconformity
North End, Littleworth, and Spaniard's End (in Hampstead), *Mdx.* ix
Northolt, *Mdx.* iv
Northover, *Som.* iii
Northstowe Hundred, *Cambs.* ix
Northwich, Sir John Deane's Grammar School, *Ches.* iii
Norton Abbey, *Ches.* iii
Norwood, including Southall, *Mdx.* iv
Nunton and Bodenham (in Downton), *Wilts.* xi
Nuthurst, *Suss.* vi (3)

Oakengates, *see* Wombridge
Oakington, *Cambs.* ix
Ockendon, North and South, *Essex* vii
Officers, Seals, and Arms, *Salop.* iii; Lists of Officers, *Yorks. E.R.* vi; *and see* Aldermen; Bailiffs
Offlow Hundred (part), *Staffs.* xvii
Ogbourne St. Andrew, *Wilts.* xii
Ogbourne St. George, *Wilts.* xii
Orwell, *Cambs.* v
Osgodby (in Hemingbrough), *Yorks. E.R.* iii
Ossulstone Hundred (part), *Mdx.* vi–viii
Oswestry: Hospital of St. John, *Salop.* ii; School, *Salop.* ii
Otter-Hunting, *Salop.* ii
Ottringham, *Yorks. E.R.* v
Ouse and Derwent Wapentake, *Yorks. E.R.* iii
Over, *Cambs.* ix
Overton, *Wilts.* xi
Owthorne, *Yorks. E.R.* v
Oxford: City, *Oxon.* iv; Castle, *Oxon.* iv

Paddington, *Mdx.* ix
Painswick, *Glos.* xi
Palaeolithic Period, *Wilts.* i (2)

Pampisford, *Cambs.* vi
Papworth Everard, *Cambs.* ix
Papworth Hundred, *Cambs.* ix
Papworth St. Agnes, *Cambs.* ix
Parliamentary Representation, *Ches.* ii; *Glos.* iv; *Salop.* iii; *Staffs.* xiv; *Yorks. E.R.* vi
Parndon, Great and Little, *Essex* viii
Patching, *Suss.* vi (1); Hundred, *Suss.* vi (1)
Patney, *Wilts.* xi
Patrington, *Yorks. E.R.* v
Patshull, *Staffs.* xx
Pattingham, *Staffs.* xx
Paull, *Yorks. E.R.* v
Perivale, *Mdx.* iv
Petherton, South, *Som.* iv; Hundred, *Som.* iv
Physical Environment, *Cambs.* vii; *Salop.* iv
Physique, *Ches.* i
Pinner (in Harrow), *Mdx.* iv
Pipehill (in Wall in Lichfield), *Staffs.* xiv
Pitney, *Som.* iii; Hundred, *Som.* iii
Place-Names, *Staffs.* xiv; Roman, *Cambs.* vii
Plate, *see* Arms; Officers
Politics, *Ches.* ii; *Yorks. E.R.* vi
Population, *Glos.* iv; *Staffs.* xiv; *Yorks. E.R.* vi; Tables of, *Ches.* ii; *Salop.* ii
Preen Priory, *Salop.* ii
Prehistory, *Ches.* i; *Wilts.* i (2)
Prescote (in Cropredy), *Oxon.* x
Preshute, *Wilts.* xii
Preston, *Yorks. E.R.* v
Preston upon the Weald Moors, *Salop.* xi
Protestant Nonconformity, *Ches.* iii; *Glos.* iv; *Mdx.* ix; *Oxon.* iv; *Staffs.* xiv; *Yorks. E.R.* vi

Quantoxhead, East and West, *Som.* v
Quedgeley, *Glos.* x
Queen's Park and St. Peter's Park (in Paddington), *Mdx.* ix
Quenington, *Glos.* vii

Racing, *see* Horse-Racing
Raddington, *Som.* v
Radfield Hundred, *Cambs.* vi
Rainham, *Essex* vii
Rampton, *Cambs.* ix
Ramsbury, *Wilts.* xii; Hundred, *Wilts.* xii
Randwick, *Glos.* x
Rapsgate Hundred, *Glos.* vii
Ratlinghope Priory, *Salop.* ii
Reighton, *Yorks. E.R.* ii
Religion and Burial, Roman, *Cambs.* vii
Religious Houses, *Ches.* iii; *Salop.* ii; Sites and Remains, *Glos.* iv; *Oxon.* iv; *Yorks. E.R.* vi
Religious and Cultural Life, *Glos.* iv; *Yorks. E.R.* vi
Rendcomb, *Glos.* vii
Riccall, *Yorks. E.R.* iii
Roads (Communications), Roman, *Cambs.* vii; *Ches.* i
Rodborough, *Glos.* xi
Rodmarton, *Glos.* xi
Rollestone, *Wilts.* xi
Roman Catholicism, *Ches.* iii; *Glos.* iv; *Mdx.* ix; *Oxon.* iv; *Staffs.* xiv; *Yorks. E.R.* vi
Roman Period, *Cambs.* vii; *Ches.* i; *Wilts.* i (2)
Romford, *Essex* vii

Rousham, *Oxon.* xi
Rowing, *Cambs.* v; *Salop.* ii
Rowley, *Yorks. E.R.* iv
Roydon, *Essex* viii
Rudston, *Yorks. E.R.* ii
Rugeley Grammar School, *Staffs.* vi
Ruislip, *Mdx.* iv
Rushall, *Wilts.* x
Rusper, *Suss.* vi (3)
Ruston Parva, *Yorks. E.R.* ii

St. Decumans, including Watchet and Williton, *Som.* v
St. John's Wood (in Hampstead), *Mdx.* ix
St. Peter's Park (in Paddington, with Queen's Park), *Mdx.* ix
Salt: Domesday Salt-Wiches, *Ches.* i; Roman, *Cambs.* vii
Sampford Brett, *Som.* v
Sancton, *Yorks. E.R.* iv
Sandbach School, *Ches.* iii
Sandford St. Martin, *Oxon.* xi
Sandholme (in Beverley, with Storkhill), *Yorks. E.R.* vi
Sapperton, *Glos.* xi
Saul (with Fretherne), *Glos.* x
Sawston, *Cambs.* vi
Saxon, *see* Anglo-Saxon
Scandinavian Settlement, *Ches.* i
Schools, *Ches.* iii; *Salop.* ii; *Staffs.* vi
Scoreby (in Catton, with Kexby and Stamford Bridge West), *Yorks. E.R.* iii
Seals, *see* Officers
Seavington St. Mary, *Som.* iv
Seavington St. Michael, *Som.* iv
Sedgehill, *Wilts.* xiii
Sedgley Park School, *see* Cotton College
Seisdon Hundred, Northern division (part), *Staffs.* xx; Southern division, *Staffs.* xx
Selkey Hundred, *Wilts.* xii
Semley, *Wilts.* xiii
Settlement: Beginnings of, *Wilts.* i (2); and Building, *Mdx.* ix; Conditions of, *Ches.* i; and Domesday Agrarian Economy, *Ches.* i; Early, *Staffs.* xiv; and Growth, *Mdx.* ix; Roman, *Cambs.* vii; *Ches.* i; Scandinavian, *Ches.* i
Sheering, *Essex* viii
Shelford, Great and Little, *Cambs.* viii
Shepreth, *Cambs.* v
Shepton Beauchamp, *Som.* iv
Shermanbury, *Suss.* vi (3)
Shifnal Grammar School, *Salop.* ii
Shingay, *Cambs.* viii
Shipley, *Suss.* vi (2)
Shipton Moyne, *Glos.* xi
Shipton-on-Cherwell, *Oxon.* xii
Shooting, *Salop.* ii; and Wildfowling, *Cambs.* v
Shoreham, Old and New, *Suss.* vi (1)
Shrewsbury: religious houses, *Salop.* ii; School, *Salop.* ii
Sikhism, *Mdx.* ix
Singlecross Hundred, *Suss.* vi (2)–(3)
Skating, *Cambs.* v
Skeffling, *Yorks. E.R.* v
Skidby, *Yorks. E.R.* iv

INDEX OF TITLES OF ARTICLES

Skipwith, *Yorks. E.R.* iii

Smethwick, *Staffs.* xvii

Social and Cultural Activities (Social and Cultural Life), *Glos.* iv; *Mdx.* ix; *Oxon.* iv; *Staffs.* xiv; Social Life and Conditions, *Yorks. E.R.* vi

Sock Dennis, *Som.* iii

Somerton, *Som.* iii; Hundred, *Som.* iii

Sompting, *Suss.* vi (1)

Southall (in Norwood), *Mdx.* iv

Southrop, *Glos.* vii

Southwick, *Suss.* vi (1)

Spaniard's End (in Hampstead, with North End and Littleworth), *Mdx.* ix

Sport, *Cambs.* v; *Salop.* ii

Stafford: Borough, *Staffs.* vi; King Edward VI Grammar School, *Staffs.* vi

Stamford Bridge East (in Catton, with High and Low Catton), *Yorks. E.R.* iii

Stamford Bridge West (in Catton, with Kexby and Scoreby), *Yorks E.R.* iii

Standish, *Glos.* x

Standlynch (in Downton), *Wilts.* xi

Stanley, King's, *Glos.* x

Stanley, Leonard, *Glos.* x

Stanmore, Great and Little, *Mdx.* v

Stanton, Long, *Cambs.* ix

Stanton Harcourt, *Oxon.* xii

Stanton St. Bernard, *Wilts.* x

Stapleford, *Cambs.* viii

Stert, *Wilts.* x

Stetchworth, *Cambs.* vi

Steyning, *Suss.* vi (1); Hundred, *Suss.* vi (1)

Stifford, *Essex* viii

Stillingfleet, *Yorks. E.R.* iii

Stirchley, *Salop.* xi

Stockport Grammar School, *Ches.* iii

Stockton, *Wilts.* xi

Stogumber, *Som.* v

Stoke Newington, *Mdx.* viii

Stoke sub Hamdon, *Som.* iii

Stone, Alleyne's Grammar School, *Staffs.* vi

Stonehouse, *Glos.* x

Stonesfield, *Oxon.* xi

Storkhill and Sandholme (in Beverley), *Yorks. E.R.* vi

Stowey, Nether, *Som.* v

Streethay (in Lichfield), *Staffs.* xiv

Stroud, *Glos.* xi

Sullington, *Suss.* vi (2)

Sunk Island, *Yorks. E.R.* v

Sutton, Full, *Yorks. E.R.* iii

Sutton, Long, *Som.* iii

Sutton upon Derwent, *Yorks. E.R.* iii

Swalcliffe, *Oxon.* x

Swallowcliffe, *Wilts.* xiii

Swanborough Hundred, *Wilts.* x

Swavesey, *Cambs.* ix

Syde, *Glos.* vii

Tackley, *Oxon.* xi

Tadlow, *Cambs.* viii

Tamhorn (in Fisherwick in Lichfield), *Staffs.* xiv

Tamworth, Queen Elizabeth's Grammar School, *Staffs.* vi

Tarring, West, *Suss.* vi (1)

Tarring Hundred, *Suss.* vi (1)

Tax Assessments: Hearth Tax Analysis: Armingford and Thriplow Hundreds, *Cambs.* viii; Chesterton, Northstowe, and Papworth Hundreds, *Cambs.* ix; Chilford, Radfield, and Whittlesford Hundreds, *Cambs.* vi; Longstowe and Wetherley Hundreds, *Cambs.* v; Tables, *Suss.* vi (1)

Teffont Evias, *Wilts.* xiii

Telford, *Salop.* xi

Tetbury, *Glos.* xi

Tettenhall, *Staffs.* xx; College, *Staffs.* vi

Tew, Duns, *Oxon.* xi

Tew, Great and Little, *Oxon.* xi

Thakeham, *Suss.* vi (2)

Thearne and Woodmansey (in Beverley), *Yorks. E.R.* vi

Thorganby, *Yorks. E.R.* iii

Thorne, *Som.* iii

Thornton, *Yorks. E.R.* iii

Thriplow, *Cambs.* viii; Hundred, *Cambs.* viii

Thurrock, Grays, *Essex* viii

Thurrock, West, *Essex* viii

Thwing, *Yorks. E.R.* ii

Tickton (in Beverley), *Yorks. E.R.* vi

Tidenham, including Lancaut, *Glos.* x

Tintinhull, *Som.* iii; Hundred, *Som.* iii

Tipnoak Hundred, *Suss.* vi (3)

Tisbury, *Wilts.* xiii

Toft, *Cambs.* v

Tollard Royal, *Wilts.* xiii

Tong, College of St. Bartholomew, *Salop.* ii

Tottenham, *Mdx.* v

Town Government, *see* Government

Trumpington, *Cambs.* viii

Trysull, *Staffs.* xx

Twyford, West, *Mdx.* vii

Tyburnia (in Paddington), *Mdx.* ix

University of Keele, *see* Keele

Upavon, *Wilts.* x

Upminster, *Essex* vii

Urchfont, *Wilts.* x

Uttoxeter, Alleyne's Grammar School, *Staffs.* vi

Uxbridge (in Hillingdon), *Mdx.* iv

Vale of Health (in Hampstead), *Mdx.* ix

Vale Royal Abbey, *Ches.* iii

Wales, *see* Cheshire and North-East Wales

Wall, with Pipehill (in Lichfield), *Staffs.* xiv

Wallasey Grammar School, *Ches.* iii

Walsall, *Staffs.* xvii; Queen Mary's Grammar School, *Staffs.* vi; Walsall Wood, *Staffs.* xvii

Walthamstow, *Essex* vi

Wambrook, *Som.* iv

Wanstead, *Essex* vi

Warburton Priory, *Ches.* iii

Wardington (in Cropredy), *Oxon.* x

Warley, Great and Little, *Essex* vii

Warminghurst, *Suss.* vi (2)

Warnham, *Suss.* vi (2)

Washington, *Suss.* vi (1)

Watchet (in St. Decumans), *Som.* v

Waterbeach, *Cambs.* ix

Wayford, *Som.* iv

Weald, South, and Brentwood, *Essex* viii
Weel, *Yorks. E.R.* vi
Wellington, *Salop.* xi
Welwick, *Yorks. E.R.* v
Wem, Adams' Grammar School, *Salop.* ii
Wendy, *Cambs.* viii
Wenlock: Abbey, later Priory, *Salop.* ii; Liberty and Borough (part), *Salop.* xi
Wenlock, Little, *Salop.* xi
Wennington, *Essex* vii
Wessex Culture, *Wilts.* i (2)
West End (in Hampstead), *Mdx.* ix
Westbourne Green (in Paddington), *Mdx.* ix
Westbury Hundred, *Glos.* x
Westbury-on-Severn, *Glos.* x
Westley Waterless, *Cambs.* vi
Weston Colville, *Cambs.* vi
Westonbirt, with Lasborough, *Glos.* xi
Westwick, *Cambs.* ix
Westwood, *Wilts.* xi
Wetherley Hundred, *Cambs.* v
Whaddon, *Cambs.* viii
Wheatenhurst (Whitminster), *Glos.* x
Wheldrake, *Yorks. E.R.* iii
Whitchurch, Sir John Talbot's Grammar School, *Salop.* ii
Whitestaunton, *Som.* iv
Whitley Hundred (part), *Som.* v
Whitminster, *see* Wheatenhurst
Whitstone Hundred, *Glos.* x
Whittlesford, *Cambs.* vi; Hundred, *Cambs.* vi
Wick (in Downton), *Wilts.* xi
Wickham, West, *Cambs.* vi
Wilberfoss, *Yorks. E.R.* iii
Wilcot, *Wilts.* x
Wilcote, *Oxon.* xii
Wildfowling and Shooting, *Cambs.* v
Willerby, *Yorks. E.R.* ii
Willesden, *Mdx.* vii
Willingham (in Carlton, and in Radfield Hundred), *Cambs.* vi
Willingham (in Papworth Hundred), *Cambs.* ix
Williton (in St. Decumans), *Som.* v

Williton and Freemanors Hundred (eastern part), *Som.* v
Wilsford, *Wilts.* x
Wimpole, *Cambs.* v
Winestead, *Yorks. E.R.* v
Winstone, *Glos.* xi
Winterbourne Bassett, *Wilts.* xii
Winterbourne Monkton, *Wilts.* xii
Wiston, *Suss.* vi (1)
Witherington (in Downton), *Wilts.* xi
Withernsea, *Yorks. E.R.* v
Wolvercote, *Oxon.* xii
Wolverhampton, schools, *Staffs.* vi
Wombourne, *Staffs.* xx
Wombridge, later Oakengates, *Salop.* xi; Priory, *Salop.* ii
Woodborough, *Wilts.* x
Woodchester, *Glos.* xi
Woodford, *Essex* vi
Woodford Grange, *Staffs.* xx
Woodhall (in Brackenholme in Hemingbrough), *Yorks. E.R.* iii
Woodhouse Friary, *Salop.* ii
Woodland, *Salop.* iv
Woodmancote, *Suss.* vi (3)
Woodmansey, with Thearne (in Beverley), *Yorks. E.R.* vi
Woodstock, *Oxon.* xii; Old Woodstock, *Oxon.* xii
Woolaston, *Glos.* x
Wootton, *Oxon.* xi; Hundred, *Oxon.* xi–xii
Worfield Grammar School, *Salop.* ii
Worthing, *Suss.* vi (1)
Worton, Nether and Over, *Oxon.* xi
Wratting, West, *Cambs.* vi
Wrekin College, *Salop.* ii
Wrockwardine, *Salop.* xi; Wrockwardine Wood, *Salop.* xi
Wroughton, *Wilts.* xi
Wroxeter Grammar School, *see* Donnington
Wyndham Half-Hundred, *Suss.* vi (3)

Yarnton, *Oxon.* xii
Yeovilton, *Som.* iii

INDEX OF AUTHORS

THE following index is of authors', editors', and indexers' names that are printed in the tables of contents. Only a limited attempt has been made to penetrate beyond those tables. Thus if a section of an article is attributed to someone in a footnote printed in the text the name of that person will not be found in the index.

An asterisk(*) has been placed against the number of a volume in which an author's name, in the foregoing lists, is printed more than once.

Allison, Keith John, *Yorks. E.R.* ii*–vi*
Angold, Michael John, *Salop.* ii*
Atienza, A. D., *Essex* vi

Baggs, Anthony Paget, *Cambs.* v–vi, viii–ix; *Ches.* iii; *Essex* vii–viii; *Glos.* iv, vii, xi; *Mdx.* v–ix; *Oxon.* iv, xi–xii; *Salop.* xi; *Som.* iii–v; *Staffs.* vi, xiv*, xvii, xx; *Suss.* vi (1)–(3); *Wilts.* x–xiii; *Yorks. E.R.* iii–vi
Baker, Thomas Francis Timothy, *Mdx.* iv*–vii*, viii, ix*
Baugh, George Crombie, *Salop.* ii, iii*–iv*, xi*; *Staffs.* xvii*
Birrell, Jean R., *Staffs.* vi
Blair, William John, *Oxon.* xii
Board, Beryl Alberta, *Essex* vi*–viii*, Bibl. Supp.*
Bolton, Diane Kay, *Cambs.* v*; *Mdx.* iv, v*, vi, vii*, viii–ix
Bonney, Desmond John, *Wilts.* i (2)
Briggs, Nancy, *Essex* vi, viii
Brittain, Frederick, *Cambs.* v
Brown, Arthur Frederick James, *Essex* vi; Lucy Margaret, *Yorks. E.R.* vi
Browne, David M., *Cambs.* vii
Bush, Robin James Edwin, *Som.* iii*–v*

Chance, Eleanor, *Oxon.* iv, xii
Chibnall, Marjorie McCallum, *Salop.* ii*
Clark, Peter Alan, *Glos.* iv
Clarke, Celia Beatrice, *Cambs.* v
Cockburn, James Swanston, *Mdx.* iv*
Colvin, Christina, *Oxon.* iv*, x–xi, xii; Howard Montagu, *Oxon.* xi
Cooper, Janet Mary, *Oxon.* iv*, x*–xii*; Nicholas Hugh, *Oxon.* x
Cox, David Charles, *Salop.* ii, iii*, iv, xi*
Crittall, Christine Elizabeth, *Wilts.* i (2)*, x*–xi*
Croot, Patricia Elizabeth Catherine, *Mdx.* vii*–viii*, ix
Crossley, Alan, *Oxon.* iv*, x*–xii*
Crowley, Douglas Alfred, *Wilts.* x*–xiii*
Cunliffe, Barrington Windsor, *Wilts.* i (2)
Currie, Christopher Richard John, *Cambs.* ix; *Staffs.* vi*, xvii; *Suss.* vi (2)*–(3)*

Day, Christopher John, *Oxon.* iv*, xi*–xii*
Duncombe, Graham Richard, *Cambs.* v*
Dunning, Robert William, *Cambs.* v*; *Som.* iii*–v*
Durgan, Shirley, *Essex* Bibl. Supp.

Edwards, Peter Roger, *Salop.* iv

Elrington, Christopher Robin, *Cambs.* v*, vii; *Glos.* x*; *Suss.* vi (1), vi (3)

Fisher, John Lionel, *Essex* vi, viii*
Forster, Gordon Colin Fawcett, *Yorks. E.R.* vi
Freeman, Jane, *Wilts.* xi, xii*–xiii*

Gaydon, Alexander Thomas, *Salop.* ii*
Green, Judith Ann, *Ches.* ii*
Greenslade, Michael Washington, *Staffs.* vi*, xiv*, xvii*, xx*
Grieve, Hilda Elizabeth Poole, *Essex* vi*–vii*, viii

Hall, Ivan, *Yorks. E.R.* vi
Harding, Vanessa Ann, *Essex* viii*
Harris, Brian Ernest, *Ches.* i*–iii*
Harvey, Paul Dean Adshead, *Oxon.* x
Hasler, Joan, *Essex* vii*, viii
Hassall, Tom Grafton, *Oxon.* iv, xii
Hebblethwaite, Sheila M., *Ches.* i
Heighway, Carolyn, *Glos.* iv*
Herbert, Nicholas Martin, *Glos.* iv*, vii*, x*–xi*
Hicks, Michael Anthony, *Mdx.* vi*, vii
Hill, Robin Charles, *Salop.* iv
Hollings, I. Marjory, *Oxon.* x
Hook, Judith, *Oxon.* x
Horrox, Rosemary E., *Yorks. E.R.* vi
Hudson, Timothy Peter, *Suss.* vi (1)*–(3)*
Hutchings, Dennis W., *Suss.* Index

Jessup, Barbara Mary, *Oxon.* iv, x
Johnson, David John, *Essex*, vi; Douglas Anthony, *Staffs.* vi*, xiv*, xvii*, xx*; Leslie John, *Suss.* Index
Jurica, Alois Richard John, *Glos.* iv*, vii*, xi*

Keeling, Susan Margaret, *Cambs.* vi*, vii, viii*; *Suss.* vi (1), Index
Kent, Graham Henry Robert, *Yorks. E.R.* iii*–vi*
Kermode, Jennifer Isabel, *Cambs.* v*
Kettle, Ann Julia, *Ches.* iii; *Salop.* iv; *Staffs.* vi, xx
King, Heinz Peter Francis, *Mdx.* iv
Knight, Norma, *Essex* viii*

Lander, Stephen James, *Ches.* ii, iii*
Leslie, Jennifer, *Suss.* Index; Kim C., *Suss.* Index
Lewis, Christopher Piers, *Cambs.* ix*; *Suss.* Index
Liddell, Susan, *Essex* vi
Lobel, Mary Doreen, *Oxon.* x
Longley, David M. T., *Ches.* i

McFall, Jessie, *Salop.* xi*

Maloney, Monica G., *Suss.* Index

Mason, John Frederick Arthur, *Oxon.* x; *Salop.* iii

Meekings, Cecil Anthony Francis, *Cambs.* v–vi, viii–ix

Morgan, Kathleen Mary, *Glos.* x

Morrill, John Stephen, *Ches.* ii

Neave, David, *Yorks. E.R.* vi

Oxfordshire Editorial Staff, *Oxon.* x*

Parsons, Margaret Agnes, *Essex* vi, viii*

Perren, Richard, *Salop.* iv

Petch, Dennis Frank, *Ches.* i

Piggott, Stuart, *Wilts.* i (2)

Powell, Avril Hayman, *Essex* vi; William Raymond, *Essex* vi*–viii*; Bibl. Supp.

Price, David Trefor William, *Salop.* ii*

Pugh, Ralph Bernard, *Mdx.* vi; *Staffs.* vi; *Wilts.* x

Purdy, John David, *Yorks. E.R.* ii*–iii*

Ransome, David Robert, *Essex* vii*

Reaney, Percy Hide, *Essex* vi

Rosen, Adrienne Berneye, *Cambs.* vi*

Rowland, Anthony Monus, *Cambs.* v*; *Suss.* vi (1)*

Rowley, Trevor, *Salop.* iv

Rumble, Alexander Richard, *Suss.* Index

Sainsbury, Frank, *Essex* vi, Bibl. Supp.

Savell, Mary L., *Essex* vi

Sawyer, Peter Hayes, *Ches.* i*

Scarff, Eileen Patricia, *Mdx.* v

Selwyn, Nesta, *Oxon.* iv*, xi–xii

Sheils, William Joseph, *Glos.* xi*

Simms, Wilfrid, *Essex* vi

Siraut, Mary Christine, *Som.* v*

Smith, Brian Stanley, *Glos.* x*

Stamper, Paul Adam, *Salop.* iv*, xi*

Stephens, William Brewer, *Cambs.* v

Stevenson, Janet Heather, *Wilts.* x*–xiii*

Thacker, Alan Thomas, *Ches.* i*, iii*

Tomkinson, Anthony, *Oxon.* xi*

Tomlinson, Margaret, *Cambs.* v; *Essex* vi; *Glos.* x; *Salop.* ii*; *Som.* iii; *Wilts.* x; *Yorks. E.R.* ii

Townley, Simon Charles, *Oxon.* xii*

Trinder, Barrie Stuart, *Oxon.* x*; *Salop.* ii

Tringham, Nigel John, *Staffs.* xiv*, xx*

Turner, Hilary Louise, *Oxon.* x

Tyack, Geoffrey Christopher, *Mdx.* v*

Ward, Gladys A., *Essex* vii*, viii

Wardle, David, *Ches.* iii

Wilkes, John Joseph, *Cambs.* vii

Winchester, Angus James Logie, *Salop.* xi*

Worsley, Anne Victoria, *Essex* vi*

Wright, Anthony Peter Mandell, *Cambs.* v*–vi*, viii*–ix*

Wyld, Gillian Ruth, *Mdx.* iv*

Yaxley, David Christopher, *Mdx.* iv

CORRIGENDA TO THE
GENERAL INTRODUCTION

page   9, line 5, *for* 'Blow' *read* 'Bloe'

„   10, line 8, *for* 'Werwicke' *read* 'Wernicke'

„   14, line 8 from end, *for* 'Blow' *read* 'Bloe'

„   21, line 2 from end, *omit* 'two' *and for* 'No' *read* 'For instance no'

„   21, last line, *for* 'supplied ... Essex, the' *read* 'supplied.'

„   22, *omit line 1*

„   26, line 10 from end, *for* 'to a' *read* 'to'

„   29, line 2 from end, *before* '*Oxfordshire*' *add* '*Gloucestershire* VIII (1968),'

„   29, last line, *for* '1971' *read* '1970'

„   31*a, s.v.* **Cumberland** I, *for* '[no editor named]' *read* '[ed. James Wilson]'

„   31*b, s.v.* **Essex** I, *for* '[no editor named]' *read* '[ed. H. Arthur Doubleday and William Page]'

„   32*b, s.v.* **Somerset** II, *after* '649' *add* '. With index to I and II'

„   33*b*, line 14, *for* 'Kingston-upon-Hull' *read* 'Kingston upon Hull'

„   33, *before footnote, add* '1'

„   51, line 21, *after* 'By the' *add* 'late'

„   79, line 1, *for* 'North West Bassett' *read* 'North Weald Bassett'

„   94, line 4 from end, *for* 'KATHLEEN' *read* 'KATHARINE'

„   128, line 9 from end, *for* 'of Newsham' *read* 'or Newsham'

„   241, *after* 'Bolney, *Suss.*' *add* 'Bolnhurst, *Beds.* iii'

„   241, *s.v.* Boldhurst, *omit entry*

„   265*b, s.v.* Sawtrey, *for* 'Sawtrey' *read* 'Sawtry'

„   277*b, s.v.* Fowler, the Revd. Canon William Weeks, *before* '*Surr.*' *add* '*Salop.* i;'

„   278*b, s.v.* Jeffries Davies, *for* 'Davies' *read* 'Davis'

„   281*b, s.v.* Stevenson, *for* 'Janet Helen' *read* 'Janet Heather'

„   281*b, s.v.* Tait, Prof. James, *before* '*Surr.*' *add* '*Salop.* i;'